SEO Made Easy

How to Win Clients and Influence Sales with SEO

Argyris Goulas

Disclaimer

This publication is presented with the aspiration to provide authoritative, high-quality information regarding the topic and the processes analyzed within. This book is sold under the assumption that neither the Author nor the Publisher should be asked to provide the services represented within.

No part of this book may be reproduced or transmitted in any form or by any means, electronic or mechanical, including photocopying, recording, or by any information storage and retrieval system, without written permission from the Author, except in the case of brief quotations embodied in book reviews and other certain noncommercial uses permitted by copyright law.

While all attempts have been made to verify the information provided in this publication, there are no representations or warranties, expressed or implied, about the completeness, accuracy, reliability, suitability, or availability concerning the information, products, services, or related graphics contained in this book for any purpose. The points of view expressed are those of the Author alone and should not be taken as expert instructions or guidance. The Reader is responsible for his or her own actions.

The Author and the Publisher do not assume and hereby disclaim any liability to any party for any loss, damage, or disruption caused by errors, omissions, or contrary interpretations of the subject matter herein whether such errors, omissions, or contrary interpretations result from accident, negligence, or any other cause.

Argyris Goulas has been providing creative SEO writing, ghostwriting and translation services for over seven years. He comes from Greece and he speaks and writes Greek and English with ease and grace. Argyris is currently learning French as an extra language because he loves learning new things and communicating in different ways.

He has a bachelor's degree in Electronic Computer Systems Engineering from Piraeus University of Applied Sciences. Throughout his career as a creative writer and ghostwriter, he has been inspired in many instances to write a book. His first book is *"SEO Made Easy: How to Win Clients and Influence Sales with SEO"* published in 2018 both as an eBook and as a Paperback.

In his spare time, he enjoys working out at the gym, cooking, reading and exploring the world.

Find out more about Argyris: http://argyrisgoulas.weebly.com/mybooks

Facebook: https://www.facebook.com/GoulasArgyris/

Instagram: https://www.instagram.com/goulasargyris/

Twitter: https://twitter.com/GoulasArgyris

You can also send him a message at argyrisg@mail.com

Before you begin reading this book, you can claim your

SEO Plan Checklist for FREE!

If you don't know where to start with Search Engine Optimization, your **FREE SEO Plan Checklist** will help you understand the most important SEO elements.

It consists of Website and Domain Factors, On-Page and Off-Page SEO, Keyword Research, Link Building and More! Your **FREE SEO Plan Checklist** summarizes the essential things you should do to boost your rank on search engines.

Follow these SEO best practices in your **FREE SEO Plan Checklist** to increase your long-term organic traffic to your business website.

DOWNLOAD IT FOR FREE HERE
http://bit.ly/FREESEOChecklist

Table of Contents

Introduction

First of all, I would like to thank you and congratulate you for purchasing my book, *"SEO Made Easy: How to Win Clients and Influence Sales with SEO"*!

Nowadays, there are more online users that existed 5 years ago, and Internet has become a popular and indispensable tool. From chatting with friends and family using social media to researching and shopping online, the digital world is very much a part of our daily lives.

Recent researches show that the average time people spend online is constantly increasing and this gives the opportunity to businesses and companies to display their products and services and establish their digital presence.

But where do you start? The answer is simple...

Right here! *"**SEO Made Easy: How to Win Clients and Influence Sales with SEO**"* provides you all the essential information you need to know about Search Engine Optimization. This book will help you understand how SEO works and how to use it to your own benefit with step-by-step proven strategies that you can implement right away to improve your website's ranking, visibility and performance.

In each chapter, you will find an Overview that describes what is entailed in each topic and some Key Lessons Learned and Recommendations.

You will learn how to improve your online presence by optimizing your website's rank on search engines, how to use content marketing along with SEO to boost your sales, what keywords you should use and how to research them, what is your online (and offline) competition, how Online Directories and Social Media work and many more!

No matter what your current skill level is or what you would like to accomplish, *"**SEO Made Easy: How to Win Clients and Influence Sales with SEO**"* will help you develop your digital marketing skills, advance your online business performance, promote your products or services, or just learn something new.

Thanks to technology, there are several online tools available on the Internet today that can help you create an SEO plan, analyze your visitors and website, and improve your website's rank on search engines. Some of them are affordable and some of them are even free!

Don't lose any more time and get your business online! Whether it is strengthening your relationships on social media, selling your products or services online, searching for new customers or even maintaining your existing ones, it is good to build your digital existence.

Ask yourself how can potential or existing clients find your business? What are the benefits to be online?

There are multiple advantages to be online, but the short version is that when people look for specific businesses like yours on search engines, your business will appear on those search results.

You can use your website to share information about your business including your opening hours, your location and your products or services that you offer. You can also create a social media page (on Facebook, Google+, Twitter, Instagram) where you can engage with your audience, offer special discounts and connect with your customers.

We will examine each of those possibilities in the following chapters!

Thanks again for acquiring this book, I hope you enjoy it!

Chapter 1: Getting Started with SEO

Chapter Overview: *In this section, we will explore the basics of SEO, how search engines work and how search results are displayed.*

Let's start with the basics. What is Search Engine Optimization?

Put simply, SEO is exactly what it sounds like! Optimizing your content in order to rank higher in search engine result pages. By following SEO practices, you will be able to get your content listed in better positions for users who are energetically searching for relevant information.

Whenever you insert a query in a search box in search engines (like Google, Bing, Yahoo!, Ask.com, AOL, Baidu, Yandex, etc.) you get a list of web results that include that search terms, also known as keywords. Internet users frequently tend to visit websites or blogs that are at the top of this list as they comprehend those to be more related to their search terms. Websites or blogs that rank better have integrated Search Engine Optimization (SEO).

SEO is a technique that helps search engines discover and rank your website in a better position than the millions of other websites in answer to a search term. It can also help you get organic traffic from search engines. (Users that land on your web page as a result of unpaid search results.)

First of all, you need to understand that search engine is not a human being. It is rather an algorithm that is created to search for information on the Internet. The search results are in most cases demonstrated as a list of results often referred to as Search Engine Results Pages (a.k.a. SERPs).

Those results may be a combination of websites or blogs, images, videos and other types of files. Also, some search engines extract data accessible on online databases or open directories and send this information to users in real time by running an algorithm on a web crawler.

There is a significant difference between how humans and search engines perceive web pages. Unlike humans, search engines are based on text rather than graphics or sound.

Search engines are crawling the Internet, analyzing specific web page elements (primarily text) to interpret what a web page is about. Of course, search engines are more complex than that. They perform various tasks in order to deliver the search results that users see. Some of those tasks include crawling and indexing web pages, data processing, calculating relativity, and problem-solving.

This means that search engines attempt to answer the problem that users are trying to solve rather than just returning a collection of information which is relevant to the query.

As I mentioned earlier, search engines scan the whole World Wide Web to understand what is there and automatically download content which is available on web pages. This action is executed by a piece of code, also known as a spider or a robot.

Spiders follow links and "read" every page that is included in a website, and after that, they index all things they discover on their way. Furthermore, they enable search engines to identify new pages and display fresh content.

Spiders are primarily used to produce a copy of all the web pages that they have visited in order to index the downloaded content and provide faster search results.

Considering the number of web pages that are available on the WWW (over 4 billion indexed web pages), it is impractical for a crawler to visit each website on a daily basis just to see if there is a new page created or if an existing one has been modified or updated.

Crawlers then index the content of a web page by classifying the keywords and elements that best describe the page and store it in a colossal database from where it can be later retrieved.

This is where you can use Search Engine Optimization for your own benefit!

Key Lessons Learned and Recommendations:

- ✓ Building your digital presence is vital if your goal is to increase your business' visibility
- ✓ Search engines use search terms that are inserted by users to determine what to display
- ✓ SEO can help you rank higher in search results
- ✓ Spiders or crawlers scan and index every page that is available on the Internet

▶**Next Chapter...**

Why SEO is Vital to Your Website

Chapter 2:
Why SEO is Vital to Your Website

Chapter Overview: *In this section, we will understand why it is important to create an SEO strategy, what its key points are, what you desire visitors to do with your website, how you can claim your online spot and what you can do if you don't have a website.*

Oftentimes, search engines might not be able to understand the meaning of a page accurately, but if you assist them by optimizing your content, it will be easier for them to categorize your web pages properly and obtain a higher ranking.

When users look for a specific term, the search engine processes it and then compares this set of keywords with all the indexed pages in its database. If there is more than one page that includes that term (usually thousands or even millions), the search engine calculates the relevancy of each of the pages in its index and decides what to display based on different related values such as keyword density, links, or meta tags.

Of course, every search engine has its own algorithm that might change now and then and this is the reason why different search engines display distinct search engine results pages for the same search term.

If you would like to be on the first page of search results, you should create an effective strategy that complies with the latest SEO best practices.

A powerful SEO strategy should focus on optimizing your website and its content. You may have outstanding content that would under other conditions rank highly for your target keywords, but if your website is not optimized, search engines may list your website as less relevant or even penalize it for not following best SEO practices. But if you follow those practices right, it could make a lot of difference!

Firstly, you should consider what you desire visitors to do with your website when they visit it.

Will you like to be contacted? If yes, via email, phone, or through social media?
Will you like to inform them about the products or services you offer?
You just started your business and you would like them to find you locally? If yes, what is your address? A map maybe?
You just created your e-commerce store and your goal is to increase your sales through your website?

If your main goal is to promote your online presence, you should claim your online spot and turn visitors into customers. You can use local business listings, social media, your business' website or your e-commerce store, email marketing or a combination of the above.

You will probably be wondering now:

- How can I measure the effectiveness of my SEO plan? Is it actually working?
- Do I have visitors? What do they do when they visit my website?
- Are they happy with my online presence or they are abandoning my website immediately?

The answer to all of the above is the use of Analytics. Analytics provide metrics about your visitors, how they find your website and what they do when they arrive there. If you understand where your visitors come from and what people do once they enter your website, you will be able to set up a strategy and modify it correspondingly.

Would you like visitors to:

- Sign up to your newsletter?
- Get directions to your physical store?
- Buy your products or services?
- Follow you on social media?

A powerful SEO plan will include the following things:

- Setting up your goals with realistic expectations
- Use analytics to understand your visitors' behavior and measure your website's traffic.

- Keeping your content updated and complying with new technologies and the niche you work in.

If you haven't created a website for your business yet, don't worry because there are other solutions available for your case. Local directories are a great way to increase your business' online ranking without the need of a website, by appearing higher on results pages when users search for relevant businesses in a certain location.

You can also benefit from several review sites for your specific type of business where people can leave their comments about your products or services you offer. This is a wonderful way to engage with your customers and grow your relationship with them. Moreover, positive reviews will help you stand out from the competition.

As a final point, you can use social media as your online presence. There are literally millions of people all over the world that use Facebook, Twitter, Google+, Instagram and other social media pages to create their business' profile.

Obviously, we cannot skip mobile phones and tablets. An Android or iOS app might be suitable for your business as it can help you establish a unique connection with your customers and it is also an effective way to provide information about your products or services. You can update them with the latest news about your business, send them special offers and receive valuable feedback.

Keep in mind that the more locations you provide your customers to reach you online, the more chances you have to increase your visibility.

Key Lessons Learned and Recommendations:

- Search engine processes each distinct set of keywords and then compares it with all the indexed pages in its database.

- Every search engine has its own algorithm that might change from time to time.

- Creating a powerful plan that complies with the latest SEO best practices is mandatory if you want to rank high.

- Outstanding content with poor keywords will not be listed in the first page.

- Make sure that you follow the latest best SEO practices.

- Use analytics to understand where your visitors come from and what people do once they enter your website.

- If you don't have a business website, consider using local directories, social media, email marketing or even an Android or iOS app as an alternative.

►**Next Chapter…**

The Anatomy of Search Engine Optimization

Chapter 3:
The Anatomy of Search Engine Optimization

Chapter Overview: *In this part, we will examine in detail each element that influences search engine optimization, how you can set up and make your website perfect and how you can improve your online presence.*

Setting up your business' website can be challenging. So, where do you start? How should you organize your content? What type of content should your website incorporate?

There are no correct answers to those questions, but you should take into consideration what your visitors might want when they visit your website. Make sure that your online goals are clear and start formulating a strategy that will work for the type of business you have. For example, if you own a computer repair shop, you should include all the information your customers are interested in finding on your website such as working hours, online orders or requests, your location, etc.

You might be thinking now: How are my online goals related to SEO?

Every SEO factor that will be analyzed below can be beneficial for your ranking and they will also help you improve your overall website's performance.

A website consists of multiple elements such as navigation, page layout, About Us and Contact Us pages, texts, images, videos, frames, animations, and many more.

Your first priority should be your website's usability, meaning that visitors should be able to navigate and interact with your website fast and without difficulty no matter what device and browser they use. With this, ensure that your website load time is super-fast, include a mobile-friendly version of your website, and of course, provide high-quality content.

▶ **Next Section…**

Website Factors

I. Website Factors

Let's start with the key Website Factors you should consider when planning your SEO strategy:

Website Factors:

- Page Speed
- Sitemap
- Visual Elements such as images, animations, videos, frames, JavaScript
- Mobile and Print Optimization
- Server Location and Behavior
- URL Structure
- Usability

Page Speed

You may notice that page speed is first on the list and there is a reason for that! A considerable amount of visitors abandon websites that take longer than 3 seconds to load.

Design your website in a way that encompasses nothing but the most mandatory elements. Check out your website's layout and decide which elements are completely important to your visitors.

Try to avoid multiple items such as images or videos on the homepage. Sophisticated and complicated homepages can confuse your potential customers to navigate on your website.

Sitemap

Sitemaps, on the other hand, are primarily used by search engines and other crawlers to understand the structure of a website. They are in most cases in XML format which lists all pages in a single website and how often they are updated. Its structure is notably important for websites which contain pages that are not available through navigation, but only via search tools which are integrated on the website. Sitemaps can also provide a brief outline of a website's content. Keep your sitemap simple and up-to-date.

Visual Elements

Let us now talk about visual elements. Most search engines are text-based meaning that their indexes are primarily created from keywords associated with elements such as images, animations, videos, frames and JavaScript. Given the fact that images (and videos) are an indispensable part of any website, we should consider finding an effective way for search engines and users to access them easily.

Images

As I've mentioned earlier, search engines work quite differently from users because search engines do not "scan" images, but rather text. Therefore, finding the right balance between high-quality images and SEO friendliness is mandatory.

Instead of uploading an ultra HD image which takes a minute to load that affects the overall page speed, consider using an HD image which is a little bit compressed without losing its purpose. Yes, you may have to sacrifice the quality of the image to some extent, but you will still be able to use images on your website without affecting its rank on search engines.

What is important is that images should always be in JPEG, PNG, or GIF format and contain an appropriate textual description of the image.

Make sure that all images on your website use the alt attribute, also known as a text alternative for search engines. In this way, search engines will be able to understand what the purpose of your image is, and will also assist visually impaired users who use screen readers that may be interested in your products and services. Websites that omit it may be in violation of disability legislation in some countries.

Imagine alt attribute as a small description of the image. For example, if your image contains a specific product, describe it with a few words.

Moreover, try using a relevant name for each image file rather than a random one. For example, instead of using image file names such as image1.jpg, pic2.png, webimage(1).jpg, consider using names such as yourbrandname_logo.png, yourproductname.jpg, etc. that characterize each image.

In this way, image file names will have a descriptive name along with the alt attributes; search engines will be able to understand whether they are related to the terms that users are searching.

Finally, try accessing your website from different browsers, apps and devices, and pay attention to your website's images. Do they load fast and can you download them? Are they described appropriately?

Animations and Videos

Although the idea of uploading a video as part of your video marketing campaign might seem like a "wonderful" idea, it is vital to remember that it must comply with the latest SEO best practices. Your videos might not rank as high on search engines if the content is not optimized.

Animations and videos can help you promote your products and services and turn your visitors into a sale or inquiry. If you are using videos, they should be of high quality, engaging, and beneficial to the visitor in order to receive high organic traffic.

In addition, the more the text you insert into your video, the more attention you will earn from search engines. Short descriptions and video transcriptions will contribute to your video the meaningful text it needs to stand out from your online competitors.

Animations and videos work similar with that of images, but keep in mind that search engines will not help you rank higher on search engine results if your business website contains Flash videos without a textual description. Using the alt tag in this case or a description under the actual video is considered a better approach.

You should also consider optimizing your content with social media. By motivating visitors to share your content, you will have a better chance to achieve your SEO goals. When you use social media to promote your content, make sure that you alter your video titles, tags, descriptions and keywords. In this way, users will be able to find your videos with multiple terms.

Frames

Search engine crawlers have difficulties indexing websites that use frames because the URL of the page which uses various frames remains the same, no matter which of the distinct frames are open.

Nearly all search engine spiders utterly ignore those frames because they consist of client-side code. If such elements are necessary to view the correct layout of a web page, then you can imagine why crawlers may get confused with frames.

For better SEO, avoid using frames. Some users face difficulties when surfing within frames, either because the frames are complicated or because the operating system they are using cannot understand frames.

When using frames is absolutely unavoidable, always provide valid NoFrames content for visitors who cannot read framed information. The NoFrames section should incorporate content with links to the other web pages on your website so that they can be accessed without frames. Furthermore, ensure that each frame has a practical title which gives a clear depiction of the content to be found in that frame.

JavaScript

The most critical part of JavaScript's impact on search engine optimization is whether search engines can detect the content and understand its context. But, before you learn how to optimize your JavaScript, let's start with the basics.

JavaScript is a programming language used to generate interactive and dynamic content which is operating on visitor's computer and doesn't require regular downloads from your website. Websites and almost all up-to-date browsers support JavaScript without installing additional plug-ins. JavaScript incorporates an application programming interface (a.k.a. API) for working with text, arrays, dates, etc., but the language itself does not include any input-output. You can also write JS in a plain text editor!

Modern web pages consist of three major components: HTML, CSS and JavaScript. Although technology has advanced, search engines are still experiencing some problems while trying to index web pages that include dynamic content which is generated with JavaScript.

The risk here is that spiders might not be capable of interpreting the content properly and create unintended results because there is no direct access to the source code when using JavaScript.

In addition, JavaScript code requires additional time to load and is more exhaustive for the server, especially for voluminous websites, because all external resources need to be obtained.

Keep in mind that your website should always be able to assist spiders to crawl and access your website's content. If search engines are blocked from scanning JS, they will not comprehend your website's full potential. In other words, search engines will not see what the visitor sees. This can impact your website's ranking in search engine result pages.

What can you do? The most effortless way to solve this issue is by providing search engines access to the resources they require to understand your user experience.

Mobile Optimization

As we discussed earlier, when it comes to search engine optimization, it's all about following a powerful plan. SEO is the most advantageous way to bring new potential customers to your website and an effective SEO plan cannot exclude mobile devices and print friendly websites.

Let's begin with mobile optimization. Imagine your mobile website as a simplified version of your actual website. With literally millions of people using their mobile phone or tablet on a daily basis, you cannot overlook this step. A mobile-friendly website provides quite the same things like your actual website, but it is designed in a way to work appropriately on smaller screens. This is what we call responsive web design.

But a mobile-optimized website is more than that. It offers a substantial experience for mobile users and that is important because over half of all web traffic is done via mobile devices. Furthermore, mobile users tend to surf the internet looking for things that interest them and buy more than their desktop counterparts.

If your goal is to improve your organic traffic through multiple devices, you need to optimize your website for mobile. This could be a skillful method to differentiate your business from your competition.

The first step for mobile optimization is creating a responsive website design. This involves simple design, fast loading times, responsive menu and navigation, screen orientation, website search tools, great usability, straightforward e-commerce including zoomable images, order completion, etc.

Try accessing your business website from your mobile or tablet using a data connection or WiFi and see how quickly it loads. Think of you as a possible customer. Ask yourself, why am I on this website? What product or service am I trying to find or buy? Is there sufficient information about them? Can I place my order easily? Can I contact the business directly?

Ensure that your website loads instantly (under 3 seconds) and functions well no matter what device and browser a visitor use.

Print Optimization

A great number of modern websites feature a way to print some pages of a website in a print-friendly format. This includes removing navigation elements, irrelevant content and so on. Typically, print optimization requires less paper and is, therefore, greater for the environment.

The best way to create a print friendly format is by using CSS print stylesheets. These print stylesheets will guarantee that the URL is exactly the same and there is no duplicate version of each page for printing, no matter what view is provided to the visitor or search engine. CSS print stylesheets usually incorporate a style which enhances the appearance of the content when printed.

Server Location and Behavior

How important is the server location of your website? Can it affect your ranking in search engines?

The answer is 'Yes and No.' Selecting the right web hosting service can be a difficult choice. There are thousands of web hosting companies out there providing very similar services with similar rates. As I've mentioned earlier, your first priority should be your overall website speed and this includes server's performance.

If your SEO goals are to reach visitors from all over the world, your page ranking will not be affected up to a point where your server is located. However, it is substantial that your server of choice is fast and responsive. This will ensure that your business website loads right away, no matter where your visitors are located.

On the other hand, if you are targeting visitors from a specific country or location, you may choose a web hosting server location near your target audience location if there are high quality services or better server infrastructure in that location, but it is not as vital as it used to be. You can also set your targeted country with Google Webmasters Tools.

In order to boost your website's performance from your own side, try limiting HTTP requests, image sizes and insignificant plugins.

URL Structure

A URL (Uniform Resource Locator), also known as a web address, points out the location of a resource on the World Wide Web. URLs are understandable to humans and they were created to replace the Internet Protocol address that computers use to exchange information with servers. URLs also classify the file structure of the given website and they consist of various valuable pieces of information such as protocol, domain name, and path. If a web page contains a subfolder structure in its path, it may have the following format:

Hypertext Transfer Protocol + Domain Name + Subdirectory + File name

HTTP is the combination of principles for transferring files including text, images, audio, video, and other types of files on the Internet.

The Domain Name is your internet address. A good domain name should be as short as possible, simple and readable by visitors.

Subdirectories work exactly like your folders on your computer. Their structure may comprise several levels of depth but keep in mind that if you are going to use several subdirectories and subfolders, visitors and search engines should not be confused when they attempt to index your content. Having that said, you should consider using clear and readable URLs. Moreover, if you are going to upload a great number of products or services on your website, using keywords inside your URLs is considered better practice than using random names or numbers.

For example:

http://www.yourwebsite.com/products/productname.

It is understandable both by humans and search engines and it can also assist search engines to index your web pages efficiently.

As for the File name, try to avoid using page extensions such as servicename.html. Using great URL format is a skill that can give your business website a powerful boost.

It has to do with usability, which I will discuss in the next step. Remember that if it is beneficial for visitors, it is also advantageous for search engines. That is why you should use keywords in your URLs instead of generic names.

Usability

When visitors enter any website on the Internet, they expect things to function in a certain way. Let's imagine that we are using our PC and we would like to get back to the home page - the first thing we will do is to click on the logo.

Usability involves the overall visitor's experience when he or she is using your business website. When visitors are looking for your business, there's a good chance that they are using their mobile devices, especially if they are on the go. Search engines are adjusting their algorithms to this modern approach, and business websites need to adjust their design as well.

A website that provides great visitors' experience tends to generate more sales and engage with customers in a more gratifying way.

Responsive design and simplified e-commerce on your business website will give your customers the capability to purchase your products and services in just a few clicks.

Remember that SEO is about drawing attention to search engine results whereas usability refers to your visitors' experience after entering your website.

Creating a favorable and sympathetic visitor experience helps to establish a positive impression that will, in turn, promote social media sharing, bookmarking, and external linking. These are all indications that influence search engines and lead to higher rankings.

Users select and click on the websites that are probable to contain the information they are looking for in the list of websites found on search engine result pages. This is where Title Tags and Meta Descriptions can make the difference!

Most web browsers such as (Mozilla, Chrome, Opera, Microsoft Edge, etc.) use the Title Tags to designate their tabs and users tend to read the content of title tags to find the tab which contains the web pages they desire to view. Moreover, when a website is bookmarked, web browsers include the content of the Title Tags which helps users to locate the web page they are searching for more efficiently.

Meta Descriptions for each page on your business website are also mandatory because they will provide users and search engines a brief idea of your content. If they find multiple results with the same Meta Description, they will get confused in deciding which link to click.

Consider the following factors when it comes to usability:

- Can they find the information (your product or service) they are looking for on your website?
- Can visitors complete their goals easily? (E.g. buy a product)
- How many steps are required to perform simple search tasks?
- Are the elements on your business website encouraging or discouraging visitors from completing their search goals?
- How fast and conveniently can visitors accomplish their search goals on your website?

Not to mention navigation and search boxes. If you own a business website with several products or services, you should ensure that your visitors or potential customers are able to find everything they need as easily as possible, and search boxes provide that power. No matter how skillful your navigation is designed and how greatly presented your products or services may be, you should include a search function on your website because it grants the visitors the ability to move from one point to another without difficulty.

Many visitors will prefer to use your search box instead of using your navigation menu, for the reason that a distinct search and a single click may be enough for them to find the information they are searching for, rather than an unknown number of clicks via the navigation menu.

Navigation, on the other hand, has a different purpose and it has to do with internal linking and how visitors can reach every single web page on your business website. If your visitors are able to locate their desired information with ease, they will be satisfied and more likely to visit your website again for what you offer.

When you are designing your website navigation menu, think about the following:

- Is your navigation menu consistent on every web page?
- Is it easy to use and does it contain all the necessary web pages of your website?
- Does your business logo link to your homepage?

Finally, think about your content. Describe your products or services expertly and ensure that your business information is clear and accurate. Try to use titles and bullet points to help your visitors rapidly scan your content. If you are using images on your web pages, use a compressed version of them as I described in a previous section.

►**Next Section…**

On-Page Factors

II. On-Page Factors

It is now time to focus on the fundamental On-Page Factors. As you may notice below on the bullet list, the first factor on the list for On-Page search engine optimization is Keywords. Let's take a closer look at the bullet list below:

On-Page Factors:

- ✓ Keywords in Page Titles, Heading Tags (H1-H6), Image Alt Text Tag, Meta Descriptions, URL, and the Pages' Copy
- ✓ Length of the Content
- ✓ Duplicate Content
- ✓ Canonical Tag
- ✓ Internal and External Links
- ✓ Date of Last Update

Keywords

One of the ordinarily neglected factors of SEO is your business website keywords, and in this section, I will help you discover all of the possible ways to optimize your products or services or content for greater ranking and organic search visibility.

Whether your goal is to boost the SEO of your business website or increase your monthly organic traffic, optimizing your content with the right keywords should be your #1 priority.

Keywords are the most important element in SEO and selecting the suitable keywords to optimize your business website on search engine result pages is the first and most momentous step for a profitable SEO plan. If you succeed in this very first phase, your road ahead will be clear and pleasant.

Finding the right keywords and performing a thorough research in order to create a list of target keywords is crucial. You can think of keywords as the search terms which are used by visitors and search engines in order to discover your product or services. There are three major points you should consider when selecting the keywords for your SEO plan:

Keyword frequency, which is the number of times a keyword is used within the search term. It might be a better approach to include keywords that users search for most often and are relevant to your products or services, but please note that it may be a little bit challenging to differentiate your business website on search terms that are immensely searched.

Your competitors are the second most substantial point because if you own a voluminous business website, you may be able to appear on the search engine results page for greatly competitive keywords that are common. These can also include the keywords that describe your business website best. You should commit to your SEO plan in order to appear on the search results for popular universal terms.

Relevance, on the other hand, is about choosing keywords that are closely connected with what you actually offer. If someone enters your business website looking for specific product or service which is not currently available on your website, they are definitely going to abandon your website.

A powerful SEO plan consists of an intensive keyword research for your content. The first thing you need to do is come up with a list of keywords that describe the products or services of your business website. Imagine you are a visitor and you are searching for a specific item on the Internet.

- How would you describe that item?
- Is there an alternate way to find that specific item with less popular (unique) terms?

There is a dedicated chapter for that (*Keyword Analysis and Selection*) where I will examine keyword selection in greater depth. Now, let's analyze each keyword factor starting with keywords in Page Titles.

Keywords in Page Titles

Page titles inform your potential customers and search engines about the topic of the web page, and therefore, can help you rank higher in search engine results pages if you use keywords that are relevant to your content. Precise explanatory titles that use target keywords are considered best SEO practice and it is frequently convenient to have a few explanatory unique words in the title. Powerful page titles are unique, short, and under 60 characters long that describe your web pages accurately and efficiently.

Try to answer these questions when creating a page title:
What can I find on this web page?

How is it related to visitors and potential customers?

What is the main goal of this web page?

Why would a user visit this web page?

Detailed page titles can assist readers to get an idea of what to expect on the web page and search engines may use page titles' context as your search engine results page snippet. However, you should avoid keyword stuffing at all costs.

Keywords in Heading Tags (H1-Hn)

Headings and subheadings are the most valuable starting points a visitor notices in the content and they do affect SEO. Users tend to regard them more thoroughly and use headings and subheadings to conclude what the content is about. In other words, headings can help visitors understand whether they would like to keep on reading that specific web page.

Headings can be located easily if a reader gets distracted, and therefore, proper use of headings is fundamental. You can also include your targeted keywords as long as they are relevant to that web page content.

You should at least include an H1 Tag on your web page because it is the title of that web page. Keep in mind that a web page should only have an H1 Tag - all other headings from H2 to Hn can be used multiple times on the same web page if you find that necessary. Headings have a hierarchical composition, so before you use H4, you should have used H3. Of course, you can go back and use an H2 Tag after you have used H3.

The main reason for classifying your web page with different Heading Tags is to provide a friendlier presentation of your content maximizing your business website usability as well as your search engine ranking.

Keywords in Images and Alt Text Tag

As mentioned earlier, images should have an expressive Image Alternative Text in case they cannot load properly and for better SEO. This can also be another great way to include your targeted (relevant) keywords within the web page that contains images, but try not to overuse the same keywords on the same web page because you will have the exact opposite effect.

Keywords in an image are supposed to give the best description of that image so they can be understood by search engines and rank better for those specific keywords. Moreover, they can provide a better user experience that will, in turn, have a positive impact on the long-term usability and accessibility. As a matter of fact, using those image alt tags is probably the most excellent way for your e-commerce products or services to appear in image and web searches.

Keywords in Meta Descriptions

Meta Descriptions are HTML elements that specify information about a web page for search engines and visitors. Generally, they can vary in length from one sentence to a small paragraph, but they should always be between 50–300 characters in order to show up underneath the clickable links in search engine results pages.

Meta Descriptions are the second thing users tend to notice after the title, and for that reason, they should be engaging and persuasive. Think Meta

Descriptions as a brief introduction to your web page - users should have a clear idea of what to expect within the content of the web page they are about to enter.

In addition, search engines emphasize keywords in the description on search engine results pages when they match search terms and this bold text can help searchers to make their decision.

Keywords in URL

By the way, did you know that you can include keywords in URLs?

In fact, the use of targeted keywords in your URLs can boost your rank in search engines because when they index your website and a user searches for a term that is contained in your URL, it will be considered a relevant result that will result in appearing on search engine results pages.

We have already mentioned how a great URL structure is formed in the previous section, but let me add these extra 3 points:

If your business website has numerous distinct categories for products or services, try to name those categories by a unique and appropriate name instead of a generic one.

Keywords in your URLs can provide extra information to searches (as well as search engines) about your content without visiting your actual web page and this can help you stand out from your competitors.

Note that changing the name of a URL can lead to significant loss of organic traffic and you should carefully examine this factor before making any changes. In this case, using 301 redirects might be the best approach to ensure that visitors and search engines are redirected to the correct page.

Keywords in Pages' Copy

Whether crafting product descriptions, featuring services you offer on your website, your business presentation or information, or even a blog post, writing extraordinary content that converts should be your number one priority.

High Quality Content:

- is original and unique,

- is engaging, useful and informative to visitors,

- has effective and descriptive titles,

- can be scanned fast with short paragraphs and sentences, bullet points, lists, etc. to make the text readable and easy to understand,

- is using targeted keywords smoothly and naturally for better SEO ranking,

- includes images, videos and other attractive elements.

High quality content along with keywords can help you achieve your SEO goal because content marketing and SEO ranking are greatly related. There is a dedicated chapter in this book about it (*Balance between Content Marketing and SEO*), so let's focus more on keywords.

Writing compelling page copy has nothing to do with stuffing keywords in your content - on the contrary, making natural use of targeted keywords and variations has. Using equivalent terms, plural forms, abbreviations, closely associated words and expanding your keyword list is considered best SEO practice that can truly help you rank better on search engines.

Keep in mind that if you do not provide coherent topic relevance through keywords, your web pages might not be indexed properly by search engines and will end up ranking on a lower position in search engine results pages.

What is more, the first 200 words of your web page copy are of great significance for visitors and search engines, and by using your main keywords, it can unquestionably help you stand out to visitors who have searched for that specific term.

As we have already discussed, try to use keywords in a natural way throughout your web page copy and if you intend to include images or videos on that web page, try to describe them with a keyword, wherever possible.

You may be thinking now, how many Keywords should you use per web page? For each web page copy, you should use about one primary keyword phrase and up to two secondary. By creating content that way, your web page copy will be more relevant to the search term that users are looking for, and as a result, visitors will find it more interesting and enjoyable. Write for your visitors and not for crawlers and choose quality over quantity.

But it is not always about how many keywords you should include - it is also about how much content you should create. For example, if your competitors have a specific amount of content about that targeted keyword, you should consider creating content correspondingly. Still, the appropriate amount of content will be based on what is reasonable for that keyword. If, for instance, your competitor's product has 300 words, then you should also need 300 words on your web page.

If you are wondering how to perform a comprehensive keyword research and which keywords you should use, you can refer to Chapter 5.

Length of the Content

When it comes to the length of the content, there are some major differences between writing content for products or services and creating content for blog posts that are featured on your business website. Factors like tone, style and structure of the content all have a huge significance when it comes to writing for different means.

Firstly, you should classify the purpose of your content, and then select the best format for that goal. For example, if your goal is to enlighten your audience, then infographics and images can make a 3-page long blog post about a product you offer and more captivating than just plain text.

Bear in mind that your visitors might be constantly overwhelmed with information from their everyday activity on social media and might not have sufficient time for meaningless or tedious information.

As you read in the previous section, there is no right or wrong about the length of the content as long as you keep it informative and authentic. Additionally, you can perform a little research and take a closer look at your competitors to see what topics they cover on their website and how lengthy they are.

However, before you create content for your business website, ask yourself these questions:

- What is the purpose of this text?
- Is it of high value and expressive?
- Does it serve its purpose?
- Does it include a clear Call to Action?
- Is it to the point?

Duplicate Content

Duplicate content refers to the content that appears on the World Wide Web in more than one location. When it comes to search engines, they will almost never display identical versions of the same content. In other words, they kind of forced to select which version is most likely to be the best result and even penalize duplicate (or copied) content.

If your business website has duplicate content on its web pages, you should immediately try and fix it by making it unique because it will impact your search engine rankings.

This is very crucial to Search Engine Optimization because search engines hate completely duplicate content and if your products or services are quite similar while having the exact content on every web page, your business website might struggle to rank well on search engines in the long run.

This is happening because search engines are not capable to decide which version of the content is the original one, and therefore, they do not know which version to include or exclude from their results.

Do not forget that writing unique product descriptions is entirely different than just spinning and shuffling text. It is all about quality and if you maintain an excellent level of quality, be assured that your visitors will appreciate it.

Canonical Tag

In short, this is a way of telling search engines that a particular URL serves as the preferred copy of a web page. Using the Canonical Tag prevents problems such as duplicate content appearing on different URLs.

There are several well-founded reasons for duplicate content on your business website, and those reasons can include:

- Numerous URLs - Specifically on e-commerce websites where URLs are generated through filter options
- HTTP, HTTPS & WWW - In this case, search engines perceive http://www.yourwebsite.com, https://www.yourwebsite.com, and http://yourwebsite.com and as dissimilar web pages, and will probably index them as such.
- Mobile Website - When using a different URL, normally http://m.yourwebsite.com for the mobile version of your business website.

In these cases the content is neither really duplicated nor copied, they are just distinct URLs providing the same content. You should use Canonical Tags on all these situations to inform search engines the authentic content, and which URL should be indexed on search engine results pages.

Internal and External Links

Put simply, an Internal Link is a hyperlink that guides the visitor to another page on your website, whereas an External Link is a hyperlink that guides the visitor to a different location on a different website.

When it comes to ranking on SERPs, there are some other factors that you have to consider when planning your SEO strategy and they include Internal and External Links as well as Link Value. We have already learned that search engines scan websites by following internal and external links using crawlers (or spiders).

These crawlers usually land on the home page of a website and then start to interpret that page and follow the first link they find. By following links, crawlers determine the connection between the disparate web pages and which of those web pages contain related content.

As you may imagine, your homepage holds the greatest link value because it has the most Backlinks (I will discuss Backlinks in section *III: Off-Page factors*). This link value will be distributed between all the links detected on that home page, and it is therefore recommended linking your newly created content from your home page to other pages on your business website. This will also help spiders to understand your website's structure more efficiently as well as the relevance and the value of your web pages.

Let us now focus more on your visitors. A website with exceptional internal link structure can make your website more accessible and convenient for your visitor. In other words, more user-friendly. Your visitor will be able to navigate through your web pages without difficulty and will stay engaged longer.

The quality and quantity of your External Links are also of great importance. Adding authoritative and educational external links to your web pages will make your business website look more credible and trustworthy to your visitors.

On the contrary, adding low-quality links will have a negative effect on your website. An external link is more beneficial if it connects to a well-known and relevant website.

External Links can be a skillful way to interact with other websites and a fantastic technique to promote and popularize your content because they can increase your website's traffic and your ranking on search engines.

Your SEO plan should include an external and internal link strategy, but your first priority should be your readers and not search engines - if your visitors are happy with your content, they will be also happy to purchase the products or services you are offering.

Date of Last Update

Adding relevant content to your business website on a regular basis and keeping it up to date can enhance user experience. Besides, the more recent and related your content is, the greater it is likely to rank in search engine results pages.

Still, showing dates on your website can impact traffic and rank negatively on search engines. The solution is quite simple - you can include dates on your website and use JavaScript to hide it from search engines. If this sounds like something you cannot do, go ahead and hire a professional to do it for you.

There are 5 main reasons why the Date of the Last Update affects your ranking:

- The frequency of your updates influences how often search engines are going to visit and index your business website. This can also be your opportunity to achieve greater rankings based on the content you create.
- Creating more content means more keywords in other words, if you provide your visitors fresh and engaging content and more keywords to search engines to discover you, it will definitely influence your standing on SERPs.
- Old-fashioned content appears lower in SERPs because users will probably click on content that is fresh and new.
- The lack of content along with an outdated website can have an unfavorable impression if you are using social media to promote your products or services.
- Business websites with regular updates give visitors the feeling that they are still active and alive, and that they still care about their customers.

►**Next Section...**

Off-Page Factors

III. Off-Page Factors

Link building should be a noteworthy part of your SEO strategy because the more high-quality backlinks on given web page, the higher it will rank on search engine results pages. The number of backlinks is, therefore, a vital step that you should consider when examining the Off-Page Factors of your business website. Let's start analyzing the following bullet points.

Off-Page Factors:

- ✓ Number of Backlinks
- ✓ Link Authority and Relevancy
- ✓ Number of DoFollow and NoFollow links
- ✓ Anchor Text

Number of Backlinks

As we have previously stated, creating great content is absolutely essential if your SEO goal is to keep your visitors engaged and increase your website's organic traffic, but you usually have to do more than that to accomplish that goal. Link building and the number of your backlinks can boost your SEO and it is not as complicated as it sounds.

As you can probably guess the quality of your inbound links is more influential than their quantity and search engines comprehend these backlinks as a positive vote from other websites. There are various techniques to create backlinks and some of them include guest posts on relevant websites, developing relationships with other website owners, etc. We will analyze these techniques in section *IV. Website Promotion: Link Building.*

Link building offers several benefits and if your business website is mentioned on other websites, you can expect higher rankings on search engines, increase in organic traffic from other websites and faster indexing from crawlers. The number of linking web pages and distinctive domains hence are of great importance.

Still, not all websites are equal and backlinks from web pages with better domain authority will be a leading determinant than those from low authority domains. What is more? The diversification of backlinks matters when it comes to link building, but too many backlinks of one type or from one website may be a spam signal and have the exact opposite effect on your rankings.

The total number of your quality inbound links can also be a sign of popularity of your business website since some search engines give more recognition to websites that hold a large number of backlinks. For this reason, when search engines measure the relevance of a website to a given keyword, it not only examine the number of inbound links to that website but also their quality.

It can be more difficult for you to persuade other website owners to get them to link to your business website rather than adjusting your web pages to be more SEO friendly and this is why search engines consider inbound links as an authoritative element.

Link Authority and Relevancy

What is more powerful? A backlink from a greatly authoritative website or a backlink from a considerably related website? The answer to that question is quite tricky without identifying the subject of the authoritative or relevant link.

To put it another way, it is rather a combination of both meaning that all backlinks that contribute quality traffic to your website are good backlinks, whether they are authoritative or relevant link or neither. They are just beneficial in different ways.

Link Relevancy helps users and search engines to interpret the content of a target web page and determines whether the search terms are relevant to a given link. Generally speaking, you don't have to get links from websites identical to your business' niche as long as they have context relevancy to some extent.

For example, if you get a backlink from a website that covers articles about travelling and you provide accommodation services, a link from an article related to your business location is considered relevant.

Try to find websites or blogs that are relatively similar to your business website and examine the possibility to exchange links with their website owners. Do not buy your place on any website because you will have the opposite effect. Relevant links are significant to boost your SEO, but getting complete relevant links should not be your first concern.

Link Authority is identically crucial to search engine optimization because those links come from websites that are well-established, credible and respectable on search engines as a result of their age, status, and volume.

Unlike PageRank, an algorithm utilized by Google to grade websites in their SERPs, there is no search engine (including Google's search engine) that provides any mentions or directions as to what comprises an authority link but we can certainly make an educated guess.

The fundamental idea is that more prominent websites are probable to receive more links from other websites. Authority websites include well-known market websites, government and educational institutions, large-scale companies, etc., and that is the reason why they are remarkably difficult to get and at the same time so powerful for your website ranking.

As mentioned earlier, practically, all links are beneficial, even links with lower PageRank or lower authority as long as they are quality links - not massive links from link farms which you should always avoid.

Number of DoFollow and NoFollow Links

In theory, if you have the proper links, you may rank in search engine's top 10 results. And search engines' design has developed over the years to benefit relevant and authority websites.

As you can imagine, links connect the dots of the World Wide Web collectively, but not all links are equally important. I have already mentioned PageRank in the previous section, an algorithm that measures link value. This link value derives for the most part of DoFollow links.

DoFollow links are followed, indexed and ranked by spiders. Due to this, they transfer SEO value to a web page making it rank higher on search engine results pages.

As a matter of fact, DoFollow links enable search engines to follow them and arrive at your website. If a website owner is linking back to you with this type of link, both search engines and visitors will be able to visit you. By default, all links have the DoFollow attribute, so you don't have to do include it in your HTML.

On the contrary, NoFollow links provide a way for website owners to inform search engines not to follow links on a given web page. Another key point is that Google does not pass on PageRank or Anchor Text across these links.

Keep in mind that NoFollow links may still appear in some search engines' index if other websites associated with them are without NoFollow, or if the URLs are submitted to search engines in a Sitemap.

NoFollow links are commonly used to deal with the performance of certain types of spam, improving the quality of SERPs and preventing indexing spam content from taking place right from the beginning. You can think of NoFollow links as backlinks that bring referral traffic to your business website but with almost no link value in the eyes of search engines.

There should be a balance between your DoFollow and NoFollow links because a healthy combination of both can even impact your ranking. In addition, if you have NoFollow links on popular websites or blogs, it can be a smart move to acquire traffic with many benefits. Those benefits may include better conversions, sales and leads.

Backlinks from social media pages, authoritative websites, forums and other related websites can produce a great amount of traffic to your business website because they are not only rewarding for SEO, they are also profitable for your business, products or services.

Anchor Text

Anchor text is a clickable text that includes a keyword (or set of keywords) within a hyperlink and generally provides users expressive or relative information about the content of the link's destination. Those keywords contained in the anchor text can shape the ranking of that web page on SERPs as search engines use them to determine the subject of that web page.

Anchor texts are normally blue underlined texts that consist of visible words and other characters that link to another location on the Internet, and they are usually below 60 characters long. Still, it is possible to alter the color of the anchor text through HTML and CSS.

There are 6 types of Anchor Texts:
- Exact Match - includes a keyword that reflects the destination web page.
- Partial Match - contains an alternative of the keyword to the web page that links to.
- Branded - A trademark name used as an anchor text (e.g. Google that links to www.google.com)

- Naked Link - A URL that is used as an anchor text (e.g. www.google.com)

- Generic - Random text or phrase that is not relevant to the destination web page, such as "Click Here" or "Download Now".

- Images - Search engines will use image's alt tag as the anchor text of that linked image.

▶ **Next Section...**

Website Promotion

IV. Website Promotion

Website promotion is a combination of techniques and processes that can help you to drive organic traffic to your business website. You can make the most out of Search Directories, Forums and Special Sites, Link Building, Paid Ads or Submissions as part of your SEO plan to boost your position on search engines.

A business website is like your physical store meaning that your goals are quite similar to increase your visibility and online presence in order to increase sales. Website promotion is your key tool to spread the word about your business website. The more targeted visitors your business website receives, the greater the chance of producing sales and acquiring potential clients.

There are countless techniques to advertise your business website both online and offline, and new methods and strategies are continually showing up every day. Websites can be promoted in several ways and the most popular ones will be analyzed below. Let's start by examining the bullet list.

Website Promotion includes:

- ✓ Search Directories
- ✓ Forums
- ✓ News Websites and Press Releases
- ✓ Link Building Techniques

- ✓ Link Building Practices That Should Be Avoided
- ✓ Paid Ads and Search Engine Marketing

Search Directories

Every business website has different SEO goals. So, it is good to identify exactly what you want to achieve online. You can start by writing down your SEO priorities and determining your goals regarding your online and offline presence.

Search Directories or Local Business Listings can help users to notice that you own a business and it is also a simple way to provide information about your products or services to potential customers. To put it differently, when users are searching for a specific type of business nearby their area, your business listing will appear.

You could include information about your business such as your business name, telephone number, your address, your opening hours, your available products or services and other means of communication.

Local Business Listings are an outstanding way for local businesses to connect with potential clients in their area of operation. These listings include essential information about your business like your business name, your address and your telephone number. There might be some listings where you can upload a photo with your logo or even the products or services you offer.

Keep in mind that consistency is imperative, so don't display inaccurate information on some of those listings. Enter your business name, your location and your telephone number carefully for every search directory.

There are literally innumerable search directories to select from, but you should begin with the most established ones on search engines such as Google, Bing and Yahoo!, DMOZ, etc. You should also consider listing your business on leading Local Business Listings as they might be more industry specific.

In general, each search directory has its own registration and authentication process including a distinctive code, a voice or text message, or even an email with authentication steps, but nearly all function basically the same way. The important thing is that when you are successfully listed on their website, you will be able to update your business information any time.

If you are going to list your business on multiple local business listings, you may consider creating a spreadsheet to control your business information and make edits where needed.

Consistent and up to date listings should be your first priority - you don't want users to call a number that doesn't work or go to a location different from your current business location.

As you can imagine, it might take you some time to list your business on all those search directories, but it will be rewarding and worthwhile for your business, and your customers will be able to find you when they search locally.

You can discover additional information about Search Directories on *Chapter 13: Online Directories and Business Listings.*

Forums

A Forum is a website where users can exchange information, share their opinions, and have conversations by posting messages that are quite lengthier than those on chat rooms and saved online for a distinct period of time.

They usually consist of subforums that might incorporate various topics and threads, and users can submit their answer to any topic they desire or find interesting. In the majority of forums, users have to log in in order to reply to topics, but it is not necessary if they just want to read them.

Search engines tend to index forums. Thus, posting in forums is an excellent move to get high-quality backlinks for your business website, especially if the forum is well-established. In order to get that backlink, you have to include the link of your business website within your forum profile signature.

You can do a little research and locate active forums that are relevant to your industry or niche and register for an account. They don't have to be exclusively about your business - they just have to include topics that you can contribute to. Other forum users will be thankful that they find a suitable answer to their issue and your link within your signature will be most likely indexed on search engines. It is a win-win situation.

The first thing to remember is that forum administrator or moderator can edit or even delete your posts if they find them inappropriate like an advertisement for your business and not in line with the forum's policy.

Try to provide honest and helpful answers rather than spammy ones. That is to say, if you keep contributing, you may also become an invaluable and respected forum member with numerous advantages for your business. Not to mention that you will be able to connect with other like-minded people who share the same passions.

News Websites and Press Releases

This is another approach that may be profitable for your SEO goals, but it might also be with charge. Local newspapers and magazines can feature an article about your business, your products or services and share a link to your business website.

On the positive side, you will get a backlink from a respected and authoritative means, but on the other hand, you will probably have to pay for that type of promotion.

Nevertheless, there are many other websites that publish press releases, if of course there is something noteworthy as news, for free or for an insignificant fee. You can submit your press release about your new business that can attract many potential customers and the backlink from a well-established website will be beneficial for your SEO endeavors.

Link Building Techniques

It's well-known that link building is the most paramount skill in search engine optimization, but as you've read earlier, not all links are equal, so you need to be very cautious when setting up your link building plan.

Link Building is a powerful technique that can boost your visibility and ranking if your backlinks are of high quality and related to your business. Along with creating notable content, your visitors will be satisfied, search engines will include you in their search engine results pages and your business will sooner or later flourish.

However, link building can be challenging and the best practices are continually changing. I will explain below the fundamental guidelines regarding link building to give you a clear idea of how to produce high-quality backlinks and how to prevent common errors.

Here are 10 ways to get you started with link building:

Request Backlinks: Think about your relatives, friends, co-workers or even your clients that have a blog or a website that is relevant to your business website and ask for a backlink. Simple as that and a great place to start if you are a novice.

Establish Relationships: You may consider building relationships with industry related online communities such as forums, social media groups as well as niche related businesses and companies.

Start a Blog: You can use your blog to post articles about the products or services you offer or post other related articles about your industry that visitors will find engaging. However, you should keep it active and post appealing and well-written content on a regular basis.

List your business website in reliable Search Directories: I have already mentioned that in the previous section. A trustworthy directory not only gives you the opportunity to create a quality backlink to your business website but also includes helpful information for your potential clients.

Submit a Guest Post: There are several websites and blogs out there that will welcome you to publish your article as long as it is relevant to their niche and enlightening.

Analyze your Competitors' Backlinks: You will undoubtedly notice that your competition has some backlinks that you do not have yet. This should not surprise you - this can be an effortless way to discover what other backlinks you can obtain that are related to your industry.

Work with your Competitors: Maintaining great communication with your competitors can be advantageous for the both of you. You can exchange backlinks and develop a durable and constructive relationship.

Turn your Referrals into Backlinks: If there are users out there that have already mentioned your products or services without adding a backlink to your business website, you can connect with them and transform that referral into a backlink.

Gain your Backlinks: If your content is worthwhile and enlightening, visitors and other website or blog owners will notice that and will start mentioning your brand; the products or services you offer. This can be a proficient way to acquire natural backlinks.

Stay Up-to-date: By studying the latest best SEO practices and staying focused on your SEO goals can help you to preserve your online presence.

Link Building Practices That Should Be Avoided

Although link building can help your ranking and visibility on search engines if used inappropriately, it can impact your SEO in a negative way. Below are the 4 most overlooked points that should be avoided at all costs:

Buying Backlinks: This is actually a bad practice that can get your business website penalized by search engines. As you have already read in previous sections, if you try to manipulate search engine results pages in any way that is unnatural and it affects the actual valuable and relevant results, search engines will blacklist your website.

Amount of Low-Quality Backlinks: Search engine optimization is not about quantity, it is all about quality and having a vast amount of low quality and irrelevant backlinks can damage your SEO efforts. You should avoid acquiring backlinks from websites that have poor or meaningless status or no content at all.

Stuffing Keywords on Anchor Text: This is a common mistake that businesses and companies tend to neglect. Search engines will identify this as an intentional and unnatural tactic to rank on SERPs and index the link faster by crawlers. Make sure that there is a natural flow of your selected keywords in your content.

Systematically Exchanging Backlinks: While you can exchange backlinks with other industry related communities, related websites or blogs, if you perform it on a regular basis, search engines will consider it an unnatural way to obtain backlinks, and therefore, can impact your ranking negatively.

Paid Ads and Search Engine Marketing

The main purpose of Search Engine Optimization is to make your business website stand out from your competition and noticeable to search engines to achieve greater rankings in SERPs. However, there is an alternative method to promote your website in order to increase traffic which is referred to as Paid Ads and Search Engine Marketing (SEM).

I have already suggested some other alternatives such as Search Directories, Forums, News Websites and Press Releases, and some Link Building Techniques, but if there is an urgency to promote your website on search engines, you can make use of paid ads.

Let's talk about SEM first. Search Engine Marketing can help your business website to come into sight of users that have already shown some interest in your products or services using a set of keywords that are related to your business. In other words, SEM allows you to advertise space on SERPs.

Unlike the traditional forms of advertising, such as ads in newspapers, magazines, radio or even billboards where you pay for your ads no matter if people notice them, may or may not have interest in them, SEM works in a completely different way.

Users who click on your ads are most likely interested in what you have to offer because they are already searching for that term on search engines. That is why Search Engine Marketing is so impressive and powerful if used properly.

You may have already noticed these types of ads on search engine results pages - apart from the organic results that some ads displayed in the right column and across the highest points of those pages. You will learn more about how paid advertisements are displayed on SERPs in *Chapter 4: Analyzing Search Engine Results Page.*

Another key fact about Search Engine Marketing is that there is a great selection of types of Ads, but the following two are the most common:

- Pay Per Click Ad (PPC), where you select to pay when someone clicks on your advertisements.
- Cost Per Thousand Impressions (CPM), where you choose to pay per 1,000 impressions.

Equally important to SEM is Online Advertisements and they primarily consist of Display Ads, Video Ads, Social Media Ads, Native Advertising, Retargeting Ads and Email Marketing.

Display Ads can include banners or other advertisement types such as plain text, images, videos, popup ads etc. that are placed on websites or mobile applications. Below are the seven most common types of Display Ads:

- Plain Text Ads: They are quite similar to Search Ads which are displayed on SERPs - you can add a title, two lines of text and your URL.

- Image Ads: You can use and create your own images for this type of advertisement. These are usually banners or square images with specific dimensions that are encompassing the content or even wallpapers that appear as the background of a website.

- Video Ads: You can upload your own video advertisements on YouTube, the Display Network, Facebook and other major video partner websites and apps. Your potential clients can watch your Video Ad before, during or after the video they are currently watching.

- Animated Ads: They are very much like GIFs, but they have some special requirements about their dimensions and size.

- Flash Ads: They consist of a mixture of text and animated content.

- Mobile Ads: With literally millions of people spending many hours every day on their mobile phones and tablets, you can target mobile users using a wide range of criteria including geographic location, demographics, education, interests and many more.

- Popup Ads: These type of ads usually pop up on internet browsers when you enter a website or when you click on an object within a web page.

Social Media Ads, on the other hand, is a marketing realm that is not only compelling but powerful. They are very similar to Display Ads and can also consist of anything from a simple text or image to a video. Social Media advertising is impressive because you can target your audience perfectly.

You can even set up your social media ads yourself, or you can hire a professional to prepare your SEM campaign.

Native Advertising contains paid content that appears smoothly within the feed and it is naturally non- disturbing. In most cases, it includes promoted articles at the end of blog posts, recommended posts on Facebook, sponsored tweets on Twitter, and advertised content recommendations from content discovery platforms.

Retargeting Ads is the most excellent way to advertise to customers who already know about your products or services (or remarket). Retargeting works by tracking users who visit your website by using cookies and displaying your retargeting advertisements to them as they enter other websites throughout the internet. This can be an effective and inexpensive method that can boost your conversions because it reminds retargeted users of the products or services they are already familiar with.

Email Marketing is also a low-cost and dynamic form of advertising and a skillful technique to advance customer loyalty and increase sales.

▶ **Next Section...**

Domain Factors

V. Domain Factors

Let's focus now on Domain Factors. How much importance does Domain Age have in Search Engine Optimization? Does your Domain Name affect your ranking on search engines? What is the best Top Level Domain for your business website? How you should select your Second Level Domain. These are all frequently asked questions made by website owners. Before I answer all these questions, let's take a look at the bullet list:

Domain Factors:
- ✓ Domain Registration Date and Age
- ✓ Country/Territory TLD and SLD Extension
- ✓ Best Practices for Domain Names and Extensions

Domain Registration Date and Age

Major search engines like Google are always trying to discover modern proficient methods to differentiate spammy from legitimate websites. There is some truth behind the fact that websites that are successful or established for a long period of time have old age Domain Names.

This approach is based on the fact that website owners who register a domain name for 5 to 10 years will indicate that they are genuine and reliable.

At the same time, spammers tend to register and buy domain names constantly, and in most cases, spammy websites have freshly registered domain names with short-term intentions. Moreover, illegitimate websites are barely used for more than a year, but there are unquestionably some exceptions.

Search engines utmost goals are to give users the best possible and valid results, so it would only make sense not to display websites that may only be online for a short period of time. But does an extended registration period really help SEO?

It is all about branding and continuity - you don't want your domain name to expire and give the opportunity to someone else to own it. And by someone else, I mean your competitors who can effortlessly check when your domain name is about to expires and could be looking for a chance to register it.

If your goal is to present your potential customers a consistent online presence, then you should consider registering a domain name for a longer period of time. This will make your business website look more trustworthy and credible.

For one thing, several factors can boost or impair your SEO ranking and a greater registration time can only assist your business website in a beneficial way. Still, there are numerous factors that you should take into consideration and registration age is one of them.

Country/Territory TLD and SLD Extension

TLDs, also known as Top Level Domains, are the extensions that appear at the end of a Domain Name. Nowadays, there are over 1500 TLDs available and the most popular ones that rank well universally are .COM, .ORG, .NET, .EDU, and .GOV. These are also known as generic Top Level Domains or gTLDs.

There is also Country/Territory specific TLDs which are connected with distinguishing Countries or Territories and some of them integrate:

.AU for Australia,

.CA for Canada,

.EU for European Union,

.GR for Greece,

.HK for Hong Kong,

.CN for People's Republic of China,

.UK for United Kingdom,

.US for United States of America (USA).

You can also call these Top Level Domains ccTLDs (Country Code TLDs).

In like manner, there are niche-specific TLDs which are associated with distinctive industries, businesses, communities, arts and fashion, education, food and drink, marketing, music, personal welfare, professions, shopping, sports and technology such as:

Businesses

.architect, .auto, .company, .consulting, .boutique, .computer, .engineer, .energy, .finance, .furniture, .forsale, .investments, .lawyer, .property, .news, .online, .realestate, .rentals, .network

Communities

.bio, .chat, .church, .earth, .eco, .fans, .family, .fish, .moto, .team, .wiki

Design, Art & Fashion

.art, .beauty, .fashion, .gallery, .graphics, .jewelry, .photography, .studio, .tattoo

Education

.academy, .club, .coach, .institute, .mba, .school, .science, .study, .training, .university

Food & Drink

.bar, .cafe, .farm, .fish, .food, .menu, .organic, .party, .pizza, .recipes, .restaurant, .wine

Marketing

.ads, .agency, .auction, .bargains, .buy, .click, .marketing, .media, .press, .review, .win

Music, Video & Photo

.camera, .film, .hiphop, .live, .mov, .photos, .pics, .pictures, .radio, .show, .stream, .theater, .theatre, .video, .watch

Personal Welfare

.care, .clinic, .dental, .diet, .health, .healthcare, .hospital, .medical, .phd, .rehab, .spa, .yoga

Professions

.actor, .attorney, .builders, .cab, .car, .cleaning, .construction, .doctor, .expert, .law, .legal, .pets, .repair, .services, .taxi, .work

Shopping & E-Commerce

.book, .clothing, .codes, .coupon, .deals, .download, .express, .market, .promo, .shoes, .shop, .shopping, .store, .tours, .trade

Sports

.baseball, .basketball, .bike, .dance, .fit, .fitness, .football, .golf, .hockey, .rodeo, .rugby, .run, .ski, .soccer, .sport, .surf, .tennis

Tech & Startups

.app, .buzz, .cloud, .computer, .data, .systems, .tech, .technology, .software

As you may imagine the TLD options are endless and you can register a TLD that is related to your niche. But how should you select your TLD? Will it rank as high as the most well-known TLDs? The answer lies in the upcoming section *Best Practices for Domain Name and Extensions.*

Now that we have explored the TLD options, it is time to understand the most significant part of your domain name structure, the SLD. The Second Level domain is the domain name that we typically purchase from domain name registrars and web hosting companies.

To put it differently, these domain name registrars provide a service that allows you to register and acquire domain names which are officially recognized by Internet Corporation for Assigned Names and Numbers (also known as ICANN).

ICANN is a non-profit corporation of people from all over the world committed to maintaining the Internet protected and regulates Internet Protocol (IP) address space allocation and protocol identifier assignment across the world. Internet would be complicated if we used IP addresses instead of domain names that are readable and usually easy to remember.

An example of an SLD would be https://yourbusiness.com where yourbusiness is the SLD and the .com is the TLD.

It is vital to understand that search engines do scan the keywords in domain names as a ranking determinant, but keyword-stuffed domains are easily detected by crawlers.

Best Practices for Domain Names and Extensions

Naming your business website has its difficulties, and sometimes, the name that we desire for our business or brand is already taken. So, how should you choose your Domain Name? Which extension is the best for your industry? Will the TLD rank as high as the most leading TLDs? Will it impact Search Engine Optimization? In this part, we will determine the best practices for domain names and discuss which extensions tend to rank more easily.

Let's begin with the best practices for domain names. Here are the top five most influential elements to consider when picking your Domain Name (or your SLD):

Memorable and Noteworthy Domain Name

Go after domain names that are short, catchy, easy to write, and pronounceable. This can be beneficial for word of mouth marketing because your potential customers may wish to visit your business website promptly, but it is also vital for dealing with eloquence.

Owning a domain name that is easy to remember and easy to pronounce will help users to familiarize with your business and associate your domain name with something that is uncomplicated and useful.

Try not to incorporate numbers or other special characters which are not common in your domain name - instead, try to mix short words (or a single word if it is available) that are about 15 characters or less long.

Point out your Keyword

Placing your target keyword in your domain name may not directly affect your position on SERPs as it was a few years ago, it is still advantageous to embody your keyword for relevancy indicator. In most cases, search engines still highlight or bold keywords appearing in domain names.

Brand Name vs. Target Keyword

Sometimes, it is more essential to select your brand name over your targeted keywords because search engines do value branding more than keywords.

Relevance is Key

It is crucial that your domain name communicates the right message as your visitors and potential customers will have a better appreciation of what your business website is all about. Try to create a domain name that is suitable to your niche.

Stay Away from Hyphens

If your domain name consists of two or more words, you may think that it will be more appropriate to separate them with a hyphen to enhanced readability (e.g. http://www.your-business.com), but the truth is that hyphens may confuse your visitors when they type your website, and in rare cases, it might be associated with spammy websites. Consequently, not more than one hyphen should be used (or none if possible). Try to use http://www.yourbusiness.com instead of the version with the hyphen.

With a vast amount of available extensions, it is difficult to determine which one to use for your business website. For this reason, it is time to focus on the best practices for extensions. Below are the top five most effective factors you will explore to consider when selecting your Extension (or your TLD):

Location-based TLD

If you are targeting a specific region or location, then using a country-specific extension (e.g. .co.uk.) might be the best approach for your business website where your products or services are only available to consumers that live there. It will also help search engines understand that you are targeting a specific location and rank you higher on local results.

Of course, there is an alternative way to achieve this if you are already using a gTLD such as .com or .org and this approach includes Google Webmaster Tools. This powerful tool is designed to support this feature especially for website owners who handle multi-language or multi-regional websites and web pages. By setting up a target location, you will assist search engines to display the relevant language and region-specific version of your business website.

Target Niche

As you have already ready in the previous section *Country/Territory TLD and SLD Extension* there is an extensive range of available TLDs. This approach will emphasize your industry or niche to users, as well as search engines, and they will have a clear picture of what your business is all about. Try to be careful when using this method especially if you are unsure about which industry fits your business best.

.COM is still King

Over 75% of all websites choose .com for their website versus other popular extensions and it is the first and oldest TLD. Therefore, in addition to using a location-specific or industry-specific extension, it is greatly recommended to always buy a .com Top Level Domain.

Reputation Conservation

This is all about branding and protecting your business' reputation. You don't want your competitors or other people to purchase all other extensions for your business such as .net .org or any other less popular extensions like .sucks, .fail, .off, .bad, .lol or even .wtf in order to use them against you. Of course, buying all those extensions can be expensive.

Keep in mind that there are more than 200 SEO ranking factors in Google's algorithm, and domain names and extensions are only two of them. Nevertheless, having a clear perception of your domain name and TLD will unquestionably benefit your business website in several ways.

Key Lessons Learned and Recommendations:

- In Chapter 3, you learned Website Factors such as Page Speed, Visual Elements, what is a Sitemap, and also about Mobile and Print Optimization. You understood the URL Structure and terms like Usability.

- I discussed On-Page Factors and analyzed the meaning of Keywords, the Length of the Content, Canonical Tags, Internal and External Links and proceed to Off-Page Factors like Anchor Text, the Number of Backlinks, Link Authority and Relevancy and the Number of DoFollow and NoFollow Links.

- You are now able to understand what Website Promotion is all about and how to use Search Directories, Forums, News Websites and Press Releases. We also explored the most popular Link Building Techniques and Practices That Should Be Avoided and the meaning of Paid Ads and Search Engine Marketing.

- Finally, I mentioned Domain Factors, how Domain Registration Date and Age affects search engine optimization and we examined Country/Territory TLDs and SLD Extensions as well as Best Practices for Domain Names and Extensions.

▶ **Next Chapter...**

Analyzing Search Engine Results Page

Chapter 4: Analyzing Search Engine Results Page

Chapter Overview: *In this chapter, I will explore the main components of a Search Engine Results Page and how search engines produce those web pages.*

A Search Engine Results Page (SERP) is an inventory of web pages that are returned to users when they insert a specific term or a phrase online using a search engine. But what are the most important components of a SERP? What do they include?

To begin with, every SERP is one-of-a-kind meaning that even if users look for the same search terms on the same search engine, SERP will be distinctive and this is happening because basically, all search engines personalize user experience by producing results based on a broad scope of elements in addition to their search queries. These factors can involve the natural location of users, their browsing history, cookies, social media preferences and even more.

It is probable that two SERPs may show indistinguishable results on their web pages as well as integrate many of the equivalent results, but will frequently present profound dissimilarities. To put it another way, SERPs are invariably changing. Thanks to technology advancement and search engines that try to provide a more instinctive and sensitive user experience to internet users.

Search engines examine and index millions of websites and blogs and take into consideration numerous factors to determine the most relevant results for the given keyword or set of keywords. The first thing to remember about SERPs is that there are three fundamental forms of Internet Searches:

Educational

When users are searching for information about a given subject, search engines understand that they intend to acquire such information and display organic results in most cases without advertisements or other forms of paid results. This type of internet search is mainly informative.

Navigational

When users try to locate a particular website or product or service by inputting a set of keywords, search engines will try to incorporate a mixture of organic and paid results on SERPs that will be suitable for their query.

Interchangeable

Interchangeable searches carry immense commercial intent where users are most likely to buy a product or service especially if they include terms such as buy [product] or other keywords that express an active desire to purchase something.

Depending on the number of websites and blogs that contain a specific term or phrase, SERPs might show anywhere from a few to literally millions of results. What is important to realize is that users principally tend to focus on the first three pages of SERPs and this is where Search Engine Optimization can help your business website to a position near the top of a SERP.

There are four main components of a SERP:

Search Box

Search Box is the first element that internet users try to detect in order to be able to type their search query. Depending on search engines, there are different kinds of searches users can perform. For example, on Google's search engine, users are able to search the web (by default), look for images, videos, maps, books, news and more. Some SERPs will also present users a combination of all.

Total Pages

This displays users the number of pages indexed by search engines that match users' query. If users are looking for very common terms such as "spring," they will receive more SERPs, but they will undoubtedly not examine all thousands of SERPs.

Another key point here is that if users are not able to find what they are searching for, they will probably filter their search terms or alter their phrase to befit their objective.

Organic Results

SERPs customarily merge two types of content - organic results and paid results. Organic results are presented at the top positions and are filled with the web pages that match users' query.

Paid Results

On the other hand, paid results can be found at the top and the right of the organic results and they can include text-only, image-based advertisements or other forms of ads that are relevant to the query. In most cases, paid results seem to be almost identical to organic.

Apart from the main components of a SERP, there are some additional features supported by Google and the top 10 include:

Knowledge Card

Google features Knowledge Cards which are part of its Knowledge Graph that contains a wide range of information gathered from a collection of sources. Knowledge Graph results might include Personal Info, Movie, Episode and Cast Information, Image or Tourist Attractions Carousels, Points of Interest, Weather Forecast, Nutritional or Medical Data, Comparison Searches and more.

Answer Snippet

When popular search engines such as Google try to provide an answer to a given question which is not incorporated within their knowledge base, they may seek for that answer in their index. This generates a different category of organic results with the information derived from the target web page.

Complementary Questions

This is a collection of generated questions that Google considers to be associated to your search query. These Complementary Questions are merged into organic results and their position may differ depending on SERPs.

Image Set

There is a set of images that are displayed as a horizontal sequence of image links that may show up in various organic positions.

Video

When search engines assume that users are searching for a video, for example, on YouTube, SERP may present some videos with a thumbnail.

Extensive Article

Some search engines may suggest a section of detailed articles which are essentially identical to organic results if users are searching for universal or obscure terms. They have their own ranking standards which are different from main organic results, and each section might consist of up to three articles presented in one organic location.

Leading News

Leading News is a section of news articles complementary to a search query. It might come into sight in the top half of SERPs and embodies time and date as well as publisher labels.

Local Info

When search queries have local intent (e.g. a cafe in a specific location), SERPs will frequently include Local Info including a number of physical locations that search engines assume to be most relevant to the given keyword.

Reviews

Reviews, stars and rating information are occasionally presented for products, services, recipes, hotels, restaurants and other applicable items.

E-Commerce Results

Product Listing Ads (PLAs) or E-Commerce Results advertise products or services straightaway with plentiful data, such as pictures and price information.

Website Links

When users look for a specific brand or business website, search engines may demonstrate a comprehensive set of up to 10 website links. The full set of website links takes up to five organic spots, monopolizing the SERP.

Key Lessons Learned and Recommendations:

- There are three forms of Internet Searches: Educational, Navigational and Interchangeable.

- Search Engine Results Pages consist of four core components: Search Box, Total Pages, Organic Results, and Paid Results.

- Apart from the principal components of a SERP, there are some supplementary features supported by Google and the most popular ones include: Knowledge Card, Answer Snippet, Complementary Questions, Image Set, Video, Extensive Article, Leading News, Local Info, Reviews, E-Commerce Results, and Website Links.

►**Next Chapter...**

Keyword Analysis and Selection

Chapter 5:
Keyword Analysis and Selection

Chapter Overview: *In this part, I will discuss why keyword research is vital, how to select the right keywords, how you can expand your list of keywords, and how you can make the most out of Top, Main and Long Tail Keywords.*

Keywords are one of the most effective SEO factors for all search engines and they exist since the beginning of the Internet. Choosing the right keywords to optimize your business website is, therefore, the most critical step for a rewarding SEO campaign and if you succeed on this very first step, the road ahead will be very smooth and advantageous.

There are several methods to figure out which keywords are the best for your business website, and normally, the ultimate list of keywords is created after a thoughtful analysis.

How can you examine what internet users are searching for? Which keywords are best and most relevant for your business website? How about your competitors' keywords - can you use them to your advantage?

Now that you read *Chapter 3: The Anatomy of Search Engine Optimization* you have a better understanding of what SEO is and you are ready to take the next step - to optimize your business website with the best keywords. Just follow the following steps and you will be able to choose and create your List of Keywords, and learn how to expand, prioritize and fine-tune this list to best fit your SEO goals.

Keyword Research

The first thing for a profitable SEO plan is to perform Keyword Research. In other words, you should understand and determine which keywords your potential customers and visitors might use to approach your niche.

Which other terms or phrases might they use on search engines to look for your products or services (or similar products or services from competitors)? Are they searching for something else that is relevant to what your business website offers?

It is now time to start writing down all the appropriate keywords that match your industry. This initial step will help you to specify keywords so that you can optimize your content, your products or services to better match what your potential customers are seeking.

Once you have classified some good and relevant keywords, try to use them on search engines to examine how they are performing in relation to your business website in SERPs. How many of these keywords or phrases suggest your business website on SERPs? Are there any particular subjects that don't help your website in terms of traffic?

This first analysis will help you understand what is working for your business website and what is not, and once you have identified some inconsistencies in your SEO performance, your next step is to examine how to fix them.

SEO is a continuous effort because trends vary over time, users can alter their behavior, and search engines advance over the years. Your first priority should be to evaluate how developments will impact your business website over time and what you should do to preserve and grow your organic traffic. Keep in mind that getting a vast amount of visitors to your website is not as essential as getting the right type of visitors.

You may also create a spreadsheet with a list of researched keywords or you can also use Google or Bing Keyword Planner. You may select whichever approach suits you best to find the right keywords. Here are some extra steps you may take:

- Build Up Your List: The simplest way to create a list of keywords is to use a spreadsheet, but you can also use keyword database software.
- Collect your Keywords: Create a list or various lists that contain niche keywords that describe your business, products or services. Include terms or phrases that are relevant to what you offer. What keywords will your potential customer use to find you? What problems does your business website solve? What terms does your competition use? What kind of your potential customers does your business attract?

- Perform In-Depth Research: You can use keyword research tools to identify suitable keywords or topics related to your brand or niche to widen your list. Along with expanding new keywords, you can also detect which terms or phrases users are looking for to locate and click on your business website both in organic and paid search.

- Categorize your List: If you have a distinct list of keywords for distinct groups such as SEO campaigns, products or services, you can organize your list into major categories. Each tab may have its own singular set of keywords.

- Observation and Improvement: Evaluate your SEO results or work with an SEO expert to tweak your list of keywords and redesign your SEO keyword strategy.

- Keep Your List Up To Date: Trends are constantly changing, so review and update your list of keywords systematically.

Another approach is to split keywords into three major classes: Top, Main and Long Tail Keywords.

Top Keywords

These are for the most part one-word keywords with an immeasurable quantity of search volume and competition, for example, "fitness" or "energy." Because users' intent is everywhere, Head Keywords might not convert well for the reason that users might be looking for how to get fit, a list of local gyms or the definition of the word "fitness".

Main Keywords

Main keywords consist of 2-3 word phrases that get respectable search volume with at least 1,500 -2,000 searches per month. Keywords like "solar energy" or "solar energy for home" are examples of Main Keywords. These keywords have in most cases lower competition than Top Keywords, but can still be greatly competitive.

Long Tail Keywords

As you might think, Long Tail Keywords are long and they include 4+ word phrases that are frequently very definite. Phrases like "cheap solar energy for small home" are examples of such keywords. Even though they don't get a great amount of search volume separately when combined, these long tail keywords compose the largest part of searches online.

You should focus on Main and Long Tail Keywords as they offer the perfect balance between search volume, buyer intent and competition. Moreover, Top Keywords are extremely competitive and don't covert well.

Google and Bing Keyword Planner

Google and Bing Keyword Planner can help you analyze which keywords have High, Medium or Low search volume and discover new keywords that are relevant to your niche. You will determine which keywords are suitable for your list of keywords by inserting them into these two tools.

Both tools will suggest bid estimates with valuable insights based on factual trends and online marketplace competition if you are interested in paid ads. They will also provide information about how often a keyword or a set of keywords are searched on search engines and how their search volume alters throughout a predetermined period of time.

You can also create, save and even share your keyword campaigns on these tools, create advertisement groups and set up bids for each keyword to have a brief estimate of your campaigns cost.

These tools offer an extensive range of features for paid ads and you may select to target specific locations, filter results of keyword data, and include or exclude a set of phrases or keywords. In addition, both tools are powerful and free with no cancelation costs.

Key Lessons Learned and Recommendations:

- Keywords are one of the most powerful SEO factors.
- Choosing the right keywords is the most critical step for a successful SEO campaign.
- The first thing you should do is to perform in-depth Keyword Research.
- SEO is a continuous effort because trends alter from time to time, users can change their behavior, and search engines develop over the years.
- Keywords can be divided into 3 major categories: Top, Main and Long Tail Keywords.
- Google and Bing Keyword Planner can help you detect which keywords have different search volumes and identify new keywords that are relevant to your niche.

▶**Next Chapter...**

Quality Content vs Keyword Density

Chapter 6:
Generating Quality Content

Chapter Overview: *In this chapter, you will understand why it is vital to create a high quality content and how it is related to search engine optimization.*

It is widely known that if your goal is to be competitive in your industry, then featuring a blog on your business website can be one of the most inexpensive SEO strategies you can embrace to entice visitors and potential customers.

Still, generating a collection of powerless articles on your business website may have the exact opposite effect - if you decide to go with this approach, then you have to create and present high-quality authentic content that helps your business stand out from the competition and gets you discovered.

Let's start with the basics. What is Quality Content? How is it related to SEO?

There is a considerable difference between the meaning of the phrase "content is king" and "offering quality content" because the latter means that it surpasses the test of time and keeps visitors engaged and committed. Of course, the definition of quality may be subjective, but there are a few accepted guidelines that each blog should follow and will be analyzed below.

We have learned that high-quality content is substantial to SEO and that you should create your content exclusively for your visitors, not for search engines.

We can describe High-Quality Content as:

- Accurate and Concise: Try to include specific and accurate information about your business, location, hours of operation, contact information, products or services.
- Satisfying and Trustworthy: Demonstrate your brand's genuineness by displaying authoritative research, quotations, links, studies and testimonials. Testimonials from actual customers can promote your business website's reputation, stature and validity.
- Valuable and Enlightening: If you are going to feature a blog on your business website, make sure that the content is informational and adds value to your visitors and potential customers.
- Extraordinary and One-of-a-Kind Content: Your content should be unique, specialized and of high quality.
- Engaging: Adding images or infographics to your products or services can make you stand out from your competition. Interact

with your visitors via periodic updates, social media plugins or comment boxes. You may also ask them to provide feedback about what you offer or participate in short surveys.

- Apparent Call to action (CTA): You should have a distinct call to action in every blog post - you may ask your readers to comment, sign up for your newsletter, purchase a specific product or service you feature, follow you on social media, etc. To put it differently, you already have their attention, so you should make the most out of that moment to interact with them.

Things to avoid when creating quality content:
- Web pages with insufficient or no trustworthy content
- Camouflaging content with invisible text or links
- Unexpected or insincere redirects
- Advertising without providing value and good user experience
- Loading pages with irrelevant keywords
- Malicious behavior, phishing, installing viruses, trojans or other software for mischievous purposes
- Generic content

In addition, you may answer the following questions to determine whether your content is of high quality:
- Are the articles created by a professional who understand the subject sufficiently?
- Does the website have original, credible and accurate content?
- Are the articles free of spelling, grammatical or factual errors?
- Does the content provide significant value when compared to other pages with similar content?

- Is the content objective and unbiased?

- Is the content edited and proofread properly?

- Would visitors or potential customers be comfortable to provide their credit card information on this website?

- Is the content complete or comprehensive about the topic?

- Is the content outstanding with attention to detail and valuable to readers?

- Would you bookmark, share this content with a friend or recommend this website?

- Do the advertisements distract visitors from reading the content?

With these in mind, you can start producing quality content, but don't worry if you feel overwhelmed at first. It is natural and you will become familiar with it as time passes. Your first priority should be to provide value to your visitors, to maintain the content precise, readable and to the point.

Keep in mind that your blog can help you to communicate with your visitors and potential customers and provide your business website a place to express its story. Furthermore, you will be able to enlighten them about the products or services you offer and present them how to get the most out of them.

Not to mention that if the quality of your content is well-written and free, your readers will be happy to pay for the products or services you offer on your business website.

Lastly, think about your competitors. If your competitors have a blog, you are already losing some customers there. Your visitors and potential customers expect you to have a blog because nowadays, blogs are on the rise. Consider creating a blog to attract new readers and to introduce your business to a wider audience.

Key Lessons Learned and Recommendations:

- You can create a blog to be competitive in your industry and present your products or services to attract visitors and potential customers.

- By generating and featuring high quality, authentic content on your blog can help your business stand out from competition and gets you discovered.

- You should create your content entirely for your visitors, not for search engines.

- We have learned what describes high-quality content and the most important things to avoid when creating quality content.

- Your primary goal should be to offer value to your visitors and to keep the content accurate, understandable and relevant.

▶ **Next Chapter…**

Selecting the Best Social Media Platform for your Niche

Chapter 7:
Selecting the Best Social Media
Platform for your Niche

Chapter Overview: *In this chapter, I will analyze which social media platform is best for your niche, why it is crucial to use them, and how they can boost your business website's SEO and sales.*

There are pliant of choices out there and it might seem difficult to select the best social media platforms for your business as they are progressively being used by a vast amount of industries and niches. However, I will determine below which social media platforms are suitable for your business and how you can make the most out of them to attract new clients.

Social media are more than an innovation because they provide the tools to communicate and engage with your customers as well as broaden your audience. Lead generation and custom targeting for your ads are easier than ever, and right now, you can advertise directly to those who are interested in what you offer.

In addition, social media give you the ability to target specific audiences when you create advertisements on their platforms. But how could you target any audience before defining your ideal customer? And by an ideal customer, we mean a customer who:

- desires your products or services,
- has the capability to pay for what you offer,
- has the power to purchase them,
- is connected with your business' point of view.

With these in mind and before selecting your social media platform, you should also have a clear understanding of who your customers are. You could answer the following questions:

- Where are your customers located?
- What is the average age and gender of your target customers?
- What is their profession or industry they work in?
- Do they have family or kids?
- What are their hobbies?
- Do you offer a solution to their problem?
- How do they stay informed? Are they old-fashioned or tech-savvy?
- Which of all of the above are your most loyal customers?
- Which type of customer purchases more products or services?

Now, let's focus on your social media goals and expectations. The following questions will help you perceive the best platforms for your niche - don't forget that your social media activity needs to take place on a platform where your target audience spend their time on, in order to be as powerful as possible.

- Do you wish to create a social media presence for your business website just to be online and active?
- Would you like users to get familiar with your brand?
- Would you like to generate leads and sales with your posts?
- What audience are you trying to approach?
- Which social media do your target audience spends time on?

Social media can be a dynamic way to stand out from competition, to distribute news about your business website, your products or services, and to create engaging content to promote sales as long as you can productively manage your social media channels. It is vital to only work with what you can take care of - any additional platforms might result in a fruitless marketing game plan. Here are the top 6 best social media platforms for business marketing:

Facebook

The world's colossal social media platform with over 2 billion monthly active users and over 1.4 billion users that use it daily. Facebook has innumerable and marketing features available for businesses, and some of them include Facebook's feed, dynamic video retargeting, and paid advertising.

Of course, your decision should not be based on the vast amount of users, but how productive and profitable can it be for your business website. Still, if users and potential customers desire to find out more about your brand, there is a great probability they will search on Facebook first.

Facebook Demographics and Statistics

- 53% are female and 47% are male

- Most users are between 25-34

- An average Facebook user has 155 "Friends"

- 77% College Graduates use Facebook

- 88% of 18-29 year olds, 84% of 30-49 year olds and 72% of 50-64 year olds are on Facebook

- 56% of older adults that are online and use this platform are aged 65+ with 63% of them between 50-60

Pros about Facebook

- It connects people, business and brands.

- Provides the most targeted digital advertising platform in the world.

- You can use Facebook as your social media official presence, just like your business website is your digital presence.

- Live streaming capabilities and long posts in the news feed.

- You can share all types of online content, events, and advertisements.

Is Facebook the best social media platform for your niche? With Facebook, you can showcase a wide-ranging selection of products or services; you can broadcast live events or stories about your business and target specific audiences with its state-of-the-art advertising platform.

Instagram

A picture is worth a thousand words - that is the case with this globally known photo sharing platform. If your social media goals involve posting pictures to present your brand's story, the products or services you offer, then you should choose Instagram.

Users, customers, brands, agents, fans, celebrities who frequently love to share their content along with the appropriate hashtags can use Instagram to interact with their audience, feature their products or services, host giveaways, prizes, and other promotional offers.

As you probably already know, Instagram is owned by Facebook and it supports images, videos, stories and direct messaging.

Instagram Demographics and Statistics
- 49% are female and 51% are male
- 55% of all online 18-29 year olds in the U.S. are using Instagram
- 28% of users are between 30-49 years old
- 59% of 18-29 year olds, 33% of 30-49 year olds, and 18% of 50-64 year olds use Instagram

Pros about Instagram
- It is ideal for businesses that have visual or physical products.
- Brands can demonstrate their products or services in a visually captivating way.
- Businesses can use stories to engage users and interact with their followers via direct messaging.
- You can share visual content such as images, short videos and stories.

Keep in mind that quotes and motivational pictures usually have a considerable level of engagement, although you have to use hashtags along with your posts to increase their discoverability.

Is Instagram the best social media platform for your business? If you feature a visual product, the answer is yes. If your social media goal is to entice this audience and you have the ability to create persuasive images, you should use this platform to your advantage.

Twitter

This social media platform is gaining popularity over the past few years, and besides the fact that tweets were initially limited to 140 characters, Twitter is becoming more popular than ever. In 2017, there were more than 330 million monthly active users with over 340 million tweets per day or more than 1 billion every 3 days.

You can use hashtags to intensify the quality of your Twitter posts and your goal here should always be to expand the number of followers and engagement.

Twitter can be an influential social media platform where you can share abbreviated updates, communicate with other users and approach potential customers that may have a problem that your business can solve.

Twitter Demographics and Statistics

- 37% of internet users between 18-29 years old continue to use Twitter
- 25% of Twitter users are between 30-49 years old

- 13% of internet users between 50-64 use Twitter

- 79% of Twitter accounts are based outside the U.S.

- 37% of 18-29 year olds, 23% of 30-49 year olds and 21% of 50-64 year olds use Twitter.

- 42% of Twitter users use the platform daily

- 74% of Twitter users follow small businesses to receive product or services updates.

Pros about Twitter

- You can interact with your audience and the rest of the world in real time by sharing multiple daily short posts.

- Tweets with images or video that include at least two hashtags can be engaging.

- Your business can engage on trending matters and events worldwide.

- Twitter is used by individuals to the greatest international corporations.

- You can initiate, join, manage conversations and communicate with brands and customers

Snapchat

Snapchat was founded in September 2011 as a multimedia messaging app that started with user-to-user photo and message sharing; it is becoming a unique social media platform. There are more than 300 million monthly active users and 187 million of them use Snapchat on a daily basis. In addition, users create more than 1 million Snaps each day and share more than 20,000 photos every second.

Snapchat users use their smartphone to interact with other users by creating multimedia messages (also known as snaps) that may embody a photo or a short video with several filters and effects, virtual stickers, text captions, and augmented reality objects.

Snapchat Demographics and Statistics

- 71% of Snapchat users are under 34 years old
- 45% of all Snapchat users are aged between 18-24
- Almost 70% of Snapchat users are female
- 65% of Snapchat users upload photos
- 30% of internet users in the U.S. use Snapchat regularly
- Snapchat users spend 30+ minutes on average on a daily basis

Pros about Snapchat

- Snapchat supports direct and audio messaging, stories as well as voice calling and allows you to communicate in a sensible way.
- The content you post has a definite lifetime of 24 hours before it disappears, thus it creates a sense of urgency.
- Your business can reach a younger but profoundly engaged audience.
- Your business can create a loyal audience by posting genuine and transparent content.
- You can also create a scannable snapcode to allow users and potential customers to connect with your account without difficulty.

YouTube

This social media platform remains the most extraordinary audio-visual search engine in the world after Google (which is owned by Google). When it comes to Search Engine Optimization, this platform provides ultimate attractiveness and content optimization capabilities to promote your business website's ranking. YouTube supports powerful dynamic video retargeting and remarketing tools to expand your discoverability on other social media platforms.

Users can use YouTube to upload, watch, rate, share and comment on videos, and subscribe to other channels. There are numerous types of media on this platform including music and video clips, TV shows, short movies and documentaries, audio recordings, game trailers, live streams, educational videos and many more.

Unregistered users can also watch videos, while registered users can upload an unlimited number of videos. YouTube videos are available in a wide range of quality levels starting at 426x240 (240p) up to 3840x2160 (2160p).

Most YouTube videos are free to watch, while some premium channels are with subscription where you can rent movies and TV shows, YouTube Red offers an ad-free access to the website and exclusive content.

There are more than 1.57 billion monthly active users on YouTube with over 30 million daily active users. Moreover, users watch more than 5 billion videos per day with an average viewing session of 40 minutes. Each minute, 300 hours' worth of videos are uploaded to YouTube.

YouTube Demographics and Statistics

- 62% of YouTube users are males
- 33% of all internet users use this platform

- 75% of adults turn to YouTube for pleasant remembrances rather than tutorials or current events.

- 80% of YouTube users come from outside of the U.S.

- YouTube services 88 countries in 76 languages

- Males are mainly watching sports whereas females are mainly watching videos about beauty.

- 50 million users are actively creating content on this platform

Pros about YouTube

- It is one of the most excellent platforms to host your video content and share it with the world.

- You can create a YouTube account for free and upload as many videos as you wish.

- YouTube has a vast amount of traffic and online viewers.

- All uploaded content is searchable both via YouTube and Google

- You can use your high-quality content with engaging thumbnails to attract thousands of viewers and potential customers.

- Your brand can upload explanatory videos to present products or services.

LinkedIn

LinkedIn is great for B2B marketing and professional networking that allows you to share content about your business's accomplishments and goals. Employers or recruiters can post jobs and job seekers can share their working history, skills and qualifications.

LinkedIn allows employees and employers to create profiles and add connections to each other in a first-rate professional social network which may serve as real-world business relationships.

Nowadays, LinkedIn has more than 500 million users in 200 countries with over 250 million monthly active members and people often think of LinkedIn as the 'professional' version of Facebook.

LinkedIn Demographics and Statistics

- 56% of LinkedIn users are male and 44% are female
- 49% of college graduates use this platform
- Over 40 million students and recent college graduates use LinkedIn
- 70% of all LinkedIn users are not from the U.S.
- 34% of 18-29 year olds, 33% of 30-49 year olds and 24% of 50-64 year olds use LinkedIn
- 13% of internet users between 15-34 years old use LinkedIn
- 41% of millionaires use LinkedIn

Pros about LinkedIn

- Your business can use this platform to post authoritative reports or guides, e-books, videos and case studies.
- Your brand can connect with other groups and engage with other user's content.
- LinkedIn can be your business' professional platform to boost brand awareness and a place to be socially active.
- You can find people with a business mindset and focus.
- LinkedIn supports sharing job vacancies and career opportunities as well as promotions.

You should consider using LinkedIn if you are B2B because LinkedIn's audience has a significant buying authority of the average internet audience and it is where CEOs and executives like to spend their spare time. More and more specialists are noticing LinkedIn's power of professional networking and that number is not going to decrease.

Key Lessons Learned and Recommendations:

- Social media provide the tools to communicate and engage with your customers and widen your audience.

- Lead generation and custom targeting for your ads are easier than ever with social media platform such as Facebook.

- You can target specific audiences when you create advertisements, but you should have a clear understanding of who your customers are.

- You can use social media to stand out from competition, distribute news, feature your products or services, and create engaging content to promote sales.

- Each platform has certain features, and there is probably not only one ideal social media platform for your business.

- Your business actions and the value you provide shape the long-term results you have on social media. If your brand remains authentic and socially active, it will probably succeed.

- You should test, measure and repeat to reach your ultimate social media goal. If you don't accomplish them - you can always try another approach.

- Understanding which social media platform is best for your niche will not only save you time; it will also help you to stay focused on your SEO goals.

▶**Next Chapter...**

Tips and Tricks for E-Commerce Stores

Chapter 8:
Tips and Tricks for E-Commerce Stores

Chapter Overview: *In this chapter, we will determine which elements can boost your business website's ranking on SERPs and how you can stand out from the competition.*

There is no doubt that ranking in a higher position than your competitors on search engines is essential and if you manage to get more organic traffic for your business website, you can increase sales and reduce marketing costs. That is also why it is vital to understand how search engine optimization works.

A well-structured website can easily encourage and assist your visitors to find what they are looking for, and search engines like Google value usability as we have already mentioned in previous chapters. But which are the most compelling elements that your online store should incorporate to follow the latest best SEO practices?

Follow these tips and tricks to boost your business website's SEO and give your visitors and potential customers the best possible experience.

Remember that getting more clicks on SERPs means that you will probably get more sales.

- Consider using HTTPS for your e-commerce store. This is the encrypted update to the HTTP protocol that reduces your business website's vulnerability to attacks, helps to secure your customer information and creates a secure purchasing environment for your customers.

- Speed is mandatory for online stores - if you keep your load times under 3 seconds, your bounce rate will greatly decrease. You can also compress your images to achieve faster load times and better SEO.

- In 2017, worldwide mobile e-commerce revenue amounted to $550 billion and people who shopped online using their mobile phone tend to spend twice as much via digital means than those not buying on mobile phones. For that reason, having a business website that is mobile optimized is essential.

- Your content is just as fundamental as the structure of your online store. High-quality content that adds value to visitors will rank higher on search engines.

- Your Title Tag should be between 60-70 characters long and should always include the targeted keyword.

- Adding Alt Text Tag to all of your images will boost your online store's SEO - it also helps crawlers to understand what the image is about.

- Social media integrations and social sharing buttons can help visitors and customers to share what you offer and generate more organic traffic for your business website.

- Featuring live chat to your e-commerce store can advance your conversion rates by almost 50%.

- Creating and submitting an updated sitemap and Robots.txt file to search engines for indexing can help your e-commerce store display your latest products or services.

- Make the most out of internal links and present related products or services that other customers bought to increase sales.

- Your landing page should introduce the selling process - your business website may feature products or services that are popular or trending to engage customers.

- Create distinct categories for your products or services and include descriptions for category pages. For maximum results, each product or service should have comprehensive and engrossing descriptions.

- Optimize your call to actions regularly for specific holidays, promotions, and sales. Your brand can also create special holiday gift guides to get extra organic traffic.

- By writing blog posts even on a monthly basis, your business can generate extra inbound traffic. You can also introduce product or service reviews to showcase your assets while producing content that attracts users.

- Your brand can feature an affiliate program to get bloggers or reviewers to write about your products or services and promote them on their website or social media. This will not only generate more sales, but it will also create additional backlinks that will give your brand more authority and higher rankings on SERPs.

- Get your business website listed on review websites and applications - this approach can help you to boost local sales and drive more organic traffic to your e-commerce store.

- Encourage customers to leave reviews when they buy a product or service by sending automated email messages. This is another way to add content to your e-commerce store and an unbiased way to promote what you offer.

- Make sure that your keyword research is up-to-date and that you are using the right keywords for each web page of your business website - keywords and trends change over time.

- Perform research about your competitors and examine the keywords your competitors are ranking for on SERPS, which your e-commerce store is not.

- Use Analytics to collect detailed data about your visitors and website's traffic, track your landing page quality and analyze conversions. Fine-tune your SEO plan if necessary.

- Take a look at Amazon suggestions or Google's autosuggest feature to generate a vast amount of real keyword searches for the products or services that you offer - this is a great way to optimize your web pages for the most common searches.

- Use forums that are relevant to your niche to contribute to questions related to what you offer. This gives you the opportunity to assist users authentically and create backlinks to your e-commerce store.

Driving more organic traffic to your e-commerce store needs constant efforts. However, those efforts will be beneficial in the long run. Although all these points might sound complicated or overwhelming in the beginning, do remember that you don't have to do them alone - there are experts that can help you create or take care of your SEO plan.

Key Lessons Learned and Recommendations:

- Maintaining a higher rank than your competitors on search engines is fundamental.

- You can boost sales and reduce marketing costs if you manage to get more organic traffic for your business website.

- A business website with a satisfactory structure can efficiently encourage and help your visitors to find what they are searching for

- Follow the tips and tricks in this chapter to improve your business website's SEO and give your visitors and potential customers the best possible experience.

▶**Next Chapter...**

Different SEO Approaches

Chapter 9:
Different SEO Approaches

Chapter Overview: *In this section, I will explore the different SEO methods that you can adopt to promote your business website. I will examine the key differences between Organic SEO and Pay Per Click, White Hat SEO and Black Hat SEO, International SEO and Local SEO and understand what you can expect from each one.*

Organic SEO vs. Pay Per Click

There are two decisive differences when considering Organic SEO and PPC. The first is that paid advertisements show up at the top of SERPs and higher than organic listings is determined by SEO. The second is that organic traffic via search engine optimization is without charge, whereas paid traffic by Pay Per Click has a cost for each click.

Which one of these two approaches is the best for your business website, Organic SEO or PPC? Let's start pointing out the assets of each method and you can conclude which one might work best for your business website.

Advantages of Organic SEO:

- Discoverability in search engines for your targeted keywords places your business website in front of your visitors and potential customers in almost the same way as if you were using paid advertisements.

- Having your business website in organic results can shape your credibility when searchers are looking for your products or services. Many searchers skip paid advertisements and trust organic results.

- Increasing organic traffic offers you plentiful opportunities to strengthen business awareness and inform potential customers why they should choose you.

- Organic traffic is virtually free. However, SEO will take time and effort, and in some cases, money, but there is no direct cost for each impression or click on SERPs.

- It can produce an enhanced Return on Investment (ROI) over other established types of paid means, and it can actually boost PPC when they are combined and strategically adjusted.

- While search engine optimization needs time and hard work, it can, in general, be more profitable and efficient than most other marketing approaches for increasing brand awareness and organic traffic to your business website.

- Organic traffic is far more sustainable in long-term basis and does not diminish the moment you stop paying, unlike paid advertisements.

- Visibility in SERPs needs constant effort and time which can be an advantage and a disadvantage at the same time. Once your business website has established its rank in organic results, your competitors cannot plainly buy their way in. This can provide a strategic SEO advantage over your competitors if they depend on paid advertisements.

Advantages of PPC:

- The position of PPC ads on the SERPs cannot be missed. There are generally four advertisements on desktop and three on mobile - searchers will always notice the PPC ads even if they select to scroll past them.

- PPC ads are upgraded, meaning that there are numerous options to select from including location, website links, pricing, bullet points, and many more that influence the SERPs.

- Whether you offer a product or a service, you can use visual shopping advertisements that can help searchers view what they will be clicking on. This type of advertisement can boost your CTR (Click Through Rate) by presenting a feature which is not available in organic search.

- Paid campaigns can help your business website target the right audience - even if searchers don't buy what you offer from day one, that visibility will be worthwhile for your marketing.

- With PPC ads, you can decide how much you are willing to spend each day and specify that fixed limit.

- Targeting is easier than ever with PPC ads. You can determine keywords, specify hours of each day as well as days of the week, set up geolocations, language, demographics, and audience based on previous visits.

- PPC campaigns can be created within minutes and intensify in weeks. They are faster than organic traffic and you can start reaching the right audience (if set up correctly) as soon as they are active.

- You can keep track of what keywords are actually converting, at what percentage and cost and examine analytics to make adjustments.

- A/B testing is possible with PPC and you can determine which advertisement, landing page, or call to action is working best for your business. You can also use this information and adjust all other campaigns on other platforms.

- PPC ads if set up and managed comprehensively can become a powerful inexpensive way to generate leads for your business website.

What is the verdict? Organic SEO or PPC?

It is not possible to answer this question as each business is unique with different goals and priorities. However, you can consider a combination of both if this is something your business can handle in terms of time and cost.

Keep in mind that a small local business with little competition and a minimum requirement for leads per month could create satisfying discoverability in local and organic SERPs with a few hours per week committed to SEO. On the contrary, a brand new e-commerce store with high competition from major stores and online retailers such as Amazon, eBay or Shopify will probably need additional help with PPC ads.

SEO and PPC can become powerful if merged properly. Each one has its advantages and weaknesses, and if your business can use them both with a well-written strategic plan, you can boost your website's traffic and promote sales.

White Hat SEO vs. Black Hat SEO

What is the key difference between White Hat SEO and Black Hat SEO? Which method is more profitable for your business website and what can you expect from each one?

It is crucial to understand that both techniques can produce results. However, one can bring penalties from search engines that can easily impact your rank and traffic despite its immediate satisfying results and the other can improve your organic traffic and rank, but you need to stay up-to-date as SEO is continuously changing.

About Black Hat SEO

Black Hat SEO manipulates search engines by using tricks and plans of action to get higher rank without taking into consideration the human element. In other words, it involves strategies that are breaking search engine policies and rules to get faster results with high possibility of being penalized for using unethical techniques and blacklisted by search engines. These techniques are generally used by websites with a low-investment and high-return business models, such as retail stores or subscription websites.

Black Hat SEO techniques can involve:

- Automatically generated content with little or no value to readers.
- Low-quality backlink generation using special software or link farms.
- Keyword stuffing and duplicate content creation.
- Inserting hidden texts and links on your web pages.
- Spamming on blogs, forums and other websites.
- Creating unfavorable campaigns for competitors.

- Using hacked web pages to insert your content and hyperlinks which are undetected by the actual website owner.

- Unfairly reporting your competition for spam or black hat techniques.

About White Hat SEO

White Hat SEO uses ethical SEO methods and strategies that targets human audience rather than search engines. It involves keyword analysis and research, adjusting meta tags' descriptions, building quality backlinks, and creating content that adds value to readers. Those who prefer White Hat SEO expect to have long-term organic results for their business website as this approach requires more time and effort.

White Hat SEO methods can include:

- Setting up a detailed SEO plan.

- Creating original high-quality content that is enlightening.

- Adding rich content to your business website or blog on a regular basis.

- Performing in-depth keyword research and using relevant keywords suitably.

- Placing keywords naturally in headings, anchor texts, and web page titles.

- Obtaining relevant quality backlinks.

- Improving usability including your website's navigation and structure.

- Adding descriptions and alt text to images.

International vs. Local SEO

International and Local SEO are precisely what they sound like, but which one should your business website target? Let us first find out more about these two methods.

Local SEO Approach

For small local businesses that are based in a particular country or region, Local SEO is more favorable than International SEO. It is technically a search engine optimization approach that tweaks the targeted keywords or phrases to incorporate a specific region. This enables your business to be displayed in search queries for users who are looking for relevant terms and are physically located near your business.

Local SEO is suitable for businesses with physical locations within a specific area that only provide products or services to that area, and are not currently interested for global audience. Google Maps is an example of this idea and if your business is listed in the Places section, you can be found locally even if you don't own a business website.

It is essential to realize that business websites that set up a local SEO campaign might have greater prospects of accomplishing better rankings on SERPs for that particular area. This can also be a great opportunity to promote the business' online presence and get better exposure to local internet searchers who are looking for something relevant to your products or services.

International SEO Approach

If your brand, products or services are appealing to a global audience, then you should unquestionably consider International SEO. When you are applying this approach, you are basically targeting a set of keywords or phrases as well as traffic within a worldwide environment, meaning that you are pursuing potential customers from all over the world.

International SEO focuses on assisting business websites to be displayed on SERPs for search queries inserted from all over the world and while there are methods you can apply directly to your business website, there are also many other methods you can use to enhance your business discoverability including creating business profiles in business directories, inserting your business information to online maps and apps, etc.

This type of SEO is appropriate for businesses that operate on a greater global scale, such as businesses with products or services that support several companies or customers worldwide.

Of course, if you are doubtful whether your business could benefit from International SEO, you should consider discussing this method with an SEO expert. However, it is recommended to have an SEO plan ready for your business before applying any SEO approach.

What is the verdict? International SEO or Local SEO?

There is no right or wrong answer - it depends on your targeted audience and region. Keep in mind that if you own a local business that has an established presence in your region, then local SEO approach might be more advantageous for your business. Still, if your business is solely online and you target an international audience, local SEO can be beneficial in this case too, but not as substantial as an attentively planned international SEO strategy.

Local SEO is a worthwhile economical way to drive targeted potential customers directly to your door because searchers who are seeking for relevant products or services within your region will notice you and will be able to buy from you.

Key Lessons Learned and Recommendations:

- Paid advertisements appear at the top of SERPs and higher than organic listings determined by SEO, but organic traffic via search engine optimization is without charge.

- Both Organic SEO and PPC advertisements have their own advantages, but you could consider a combination of both if this is something your brand can handle in terms of time and cost.

- Both White Hat SEO and Black Hat SEO can produce results; however, one can bring penalties from search engines that can easily impact your overall rank and traffic despite its immediate fulfilling results, and the other can advance your organic traffic and rank, but you need to stay up-to-date as SEO is continuously changing.

- It depends on your targeted audience and region whether you need to choose between an International SEO or Local SEO approach.

- If your business, your products or services are appealing to an international audience, then you should consider International SEO. However, if you own a local business that has an established presence in your region, then local SEO might be more advantageous for you.

►**Next Chapter...**

Balance between Content Marketing and SEO

Chapter 10: Balance between Content Marketing and SEO

Chapter Overview: *In this chapter, you will understand the difference between Content Marketing and Search Engine Optimization, how they can help you increase the discoverability of your business website and boost turn visitors into sales.*

Some businesses might think that content marketing eliminates the need for SEO while others believe that SEO can be as powerful without content marketing, but the truth is that they are both wrong.

Finding the right balance between SEO and content marketing is essential when your goal is to promote sales and increase discoverability on SERPs. But how can these two elements help your business website? Can they work together effectively? Let's start by understanding each one individually.

To begin with, SEO refers to a strategy you follow to get a higher rank for relevant terms on search engine results pages and it various distinct approaches, including on-page and off-page optimization, website and domain factors, keyword research and website promotion, etc. All of these methods work together to assist your business website in ranking well when searchers insert keywords or phrases related to your niche into search engines.

Content marketing, on the other hand, involves creating web pages with content on your website that your readers will find interesting and engaging. Content marketing basically makes the most of those web pages to turn visitors into potential customers and sales. The kind of content you create depends on your targeted audience and your SEO goals and it can consist of blog posts and articles, product reviews and guides, infographics, videos, and many more.

It is about generating quality content and embodying keywords within the content you create that can result in higher ranking on SERPs and greater organic traffic for your business website.

Content Marketing introduces an effortless opportunity to embody specific keywords throughout your business website or target niches that would be engaging to your targeted audience. That type of content can help you to add new web pages that can be in turn ranked and indexed.

While quantity is not sufficient to boost your current rank on SERPs, this might give you extra potential spots on search engines and a more diversified scope of keywords to rank for. This can also be a great way to improve your business website's authority, which will enhance your overall SEO. Keep in mind that comprehensive, beneficial content attracts more backlinks and shares on social media that can increase organic traffic.

The relationship between Content Marketing and SEO can be considered collective and supplementary and that is why there is a noticeable overlap between these two. Of course, there are indeed differences between SEO and Content Marketing, but the only way to ensure the success of the latter is to apply SEO methods on your business website. It is vital to realize that SEO can help your Content Marketing strategy and vice versa.

There is no powerful SEO without compelling content. SEO requires keywords, but you cannot use them without content. Simple as that. You can also think of SEO as the technical requirements and content marketing as the pathway to promote the products or services you offer.

We have already mentioned that you can use a blog to publish articles related to your industry, reviews and videos on how to use your products or services. Include announcements and news about your brand, as well as special offers and upcoming events.

The truth is that search engine optimization is essentially focusing on search engines and getting greater ranking, while content marketing is focusing on engaging users by using appealing content and improving user experience, which, in turn, reflects on SEO.

If your goal is to create a complete online strategy, you will undoubtedly need both SEO and content marketing working in harmony with one another.

Key Lessons Learned and Recommendations:

- Finding the right balance between SEO and Content Marketing is vital if you desire to boost sales and increase discoverability on search engines.

- Content marketing is all about creating web pages with high-quality content with selected keywords that your readers will find informational and engaging.

- The type of content you produce depends on your targeted audience and your SEO goals.

- High-quality enlightening content attracts more backlinks and shares on social media that can in turn increase organic traffic.

- The relationship between Content Marketing and SEO can be considered collective and supplementary and that is why there is a noticeable overlap between these two.

- You can also think of SEO as the technical requirements and content marketing as the pathway to promote the products or services you offer.

- There is no effective SEO without influential content and vice versa.

▶**Next Chapter...**

Understanding Your Competition

Chapter 11: Understanding Your Competition

Chapter Overview: *In this section, I will analyze why it is crucial to understand your competition, the difference between direct and indirect competition and the points to consider when analyzing your competitors.*

A clear interpretation of your competitors might be the decisive point between failure and success. Even if your products or services focus on a unique market, there will always be other businesses offering something comparable that satisfy the same customer's demands.

For that reason, it is essential to understand what makes customers to select one of your products or services over other identical products or services from your competition. In addition, your brand should limit its preferences and determine which niche, products or services, locations, distribution mechanisms, etc., to compete. Without this knowledge, your online and offline goals will not be as compelling and productive and what you offer will have a hard time to stand out.

It is crucial to realize that all businesses face some kind of competition, direct or indirect and you should always be ready to deal with new alternative or complementary products or services from your competitors that can make your own outdated and superfluous.

When we are referring to direct competition, we mean that a great number of businesses offer identical products or services and that customers will probably analyze a wide range of aspects when deciding where to buy a specific product or service including price, value, location, quality of customer service, and product or service features. Keep in mind that different consumers will select a divergent mixture of options, and by offering this combination of choices, your business will be able to approach a unique kind of customer.

Indirect competition, on the other hand, occurs when there are businesses that feature somewhat contrasting products or services but target the same audience in order to satisfy the same needs. Nearly all businesses deal with some kind of indirect competition, but if you can examine all the possible ways to gratify their demands and create a powerful strategy, you will be able to have the edge over your competitors who might think that they are one-of-a-kind and with no indirect competitors. This is the reason why it is vital to identify all types of competition when creating your online and offline marketing plan for your business.

You can use this knowledge to produce online and offline marketing strategies that take advantage of your competitors' lack of insight and boost your own business efficiency. You can also evaluate any potential threats from new rivals to your industry and from your present competition.

Try to answer the following questions to understand your competition better:

- What products or services they offer and what is their marketing strategy?
- How about the prices they charge?
- How they distribute their products or services?
- Do they use local newspapers, radio, TV and any other means to advertise what they offer?
- Do they have a social media presence?
- Do they have a business website?
- How do they present their products or services?
- How they handle their customers?
- What type of customers do they have?
- Are there are any long-term and returning customers?
- What are their plans for the future?
- What financial resources do they hold?
- Do they have an annual report in their website?
- Do they attend exhibitions and trade fairs?

If you examine all these points, you will be able to create an effective online and offline marketing strategy for your business. Please note that you can always communicate directly with your competitors and have a friendly business talk, after all, they are not your enemies - they are just who you compete with. Do not overthink about who your competitors are - just be genuine and offer high-quality products or services.

Key Lessons Learned and Recommendations:

- A clear understanding of your competition might be the definite point between failure and success.

- It is vital to analyze what makes customers to choose one of your products or services over other identical products or services from your competitors.

- All businesses face some kind of competition, direct or indirect.

- You can adjust your online and offline marketing strategies and boost your own business efficiency by analyzing your competition. You can also examine whether there are any potential threats from new rivals to your industry and from your present competition.

▶ **Next Chapter...**

Evaluation of Existing SEO Results

Chapter 12: Evaluation of Existing SEO Results

Chapter Overview: *In this chapter, we will learn how to measure the success of our SEO plan, the factors to examine to evaluate your existing SEO results and what you can do to improve them.*

In order to determine whether your SEO strategy is successful, you need to evaluate how your business website was performing prior your SEO strategy implementation and what results you have achieved afterward. In this section, we will take a closer look at your SEO results and discover ways to assess them.

Evaluation of existing SEO results can be challenging to define as there are numerous independent as well as reliant factors such as on-page and off-page optimization, website elements, domain factors, keyword rankings, organic search traffic, etc., to take into consideration. However, you can examine the following factors to analyze your SEO performance and decide whether your current results are satisfying.

Is your overall organic search traffic sufficient?

This is a simple way to determine whether there are enough users who discovered your business website on SERPs and actually clicked on your link to visit you. You can also measure how many web pages of your business website have obtained organic traffic and how productively you are optimizing each page of your website.

How many users found your business website via backlinks?
If your link building plan is efficient by obtaining high-quality backlinks with engaging content on authority websites, your website's traffic through backlinks and referrals should grow steadily over time.

Did your rankings improve on search engines for specific keywords?
If you have detected a significant change on your current rankings, this can be a signal that there are new rivals in your industry competing the same keywords or that you should modify your current keyword strategy to other more competitive terms. Moreover, you can look at the unique visitors you get on a weekly or monthly basis and decide whether you need to alter your SEO plan.

How many backlinks are pointing to your business website?
As your brand gains reputation and authority, your content will normally appeal to other niche-related websites. However, you should always examine the quality and quantity of these backlinks.

Is your content appealing to your target audience?
This can help you analyze your content performance and evaluate whether you are driving more organic traffic to your business website. You can use social media metrics or Google Analytics as your guide to figure out which topics are more engaging than others and fine-tune your plan accordingly.

How much time do your readers spend on your business website and how many web pages are they viewing? Another important factor to consider is the amount of time your readers are spending on your web pages because this will give you a clear idea whether your content is alluring. Don't forget that the more web pages readers are viewing after arriving at your website, the more appealing your business website is, and this is uniquely important if you consider that your content should be meant for users - not search engines.

How many likes and shares do your business website receive on social media platforms?

Receiving a considerable number of social shares and likes can boost your business website's rankings indirectly as this can be an indication of your content's effectiveness and discoverability. Track down the content with the most social shares and likes, and analyze how those metrics increase over time.

Is your e-commerce conversion rate developing invariably?

The number of sales you had gained through your organic traffic can give you an estimate of your brand's efficiency even though it is not directly related to SEO.

How much does your brand invest on paid ads and promotion?

This can be another way to determine how powerful your existing SEO plan is and whether this amount is appropriate for your results.

Keep in mind that the success of your SEO strategy depends on your current SEO goals. For this reason, it is essential to specify your goals, analyze the metrics that are most important to you and find out whether your SEO plan was a success and what you can do to improve it.

Every SEO strategy incorporates some approaches that are more powerful than others, but the key to determine the success of your SEO strategy is not just to measure whether your plan has been successful in general but rather to detect which elements have proven advantageous for your business. This can help your brand to focus more on the strategies that are working for your business, and to modify or remove those that haven't with new approaches.

Key Lessons Learned and Recommendations:

- You need to analyze how your business website was performing prior your SEO strategy implementation and what results you have achieved afterward in order to determine whether your current SEO strategy is successful.
- Evaluation of existing SEO results can be challenging to define as there are numerous independent and reliant factors.
- It is crucial to specify your goals, examine the metrics that are most important to you and identify whether your SEO plan needs any modifications.

Final Thoughts - Conclusion

Search Engine Optimization can be challenging and it requires a never-ending effort as best practices are evolving and alternating each year. However, you don't need to follow each and every state-of-the-art strategy in order to stay up-to-date, you just need to have an overall understanding of how SEO works and modify your current plans of action if you notice that they are no longer productive and profitable. Bear in mind that you can always hire an SEO professional who is aware of the latest developments if you don't have the time to educate yourself.

Although there are plentiful online resources where you can seek advice about SEO, please do note that some blogs and websites are far more authoritative and truthful than others. For this reason, I strongly recommend you not to count on everything you read - you should rather test, refine and repeat. Another key point often overlooked is that all brands and business websites are unique with their own SEO and marketing goals. Thus a strategy that is successful for one business might not work for another.

I truly hope this book has been a valuable resource to you. My ultimate goal was to help by educating businesses about the fundamentals of SEO, to prepare them for the digital world and how to use SEO to boost sales and have the edge over the competition.

Note from the Author

Reviews are like gold to authors! If you have enjoyed this book, would you consider rating and reviewing it? I will be forever grateful if you take the time to leave a review on any of the following platforms: *Amazon, Goodreads, iBooks, Barnes & Noble, Kobo, Inktera, Playster, Scribd, Tolino, 24Symbols, or OverDrive.*

Reviews can help other enthusiastic readers like you to discover the authors you love, and each and every review supports authors on their journey to bring you more educational books! A review doesn't need to be lengthy or comprehensive - just honest and authentic! I'm so pleased for each and every one of you!

If you enjoyed this book, please encourage your friends and co-workers to download their own copy from their favorite authorized retailer. Thank you very much for your support.

Extra SEO Tips & Tricks

I have already analyzed numerous optimization tips and tricks on all previous chapters, but in this section, I will reveal a few more. As you have already realized Search Engine Optimization is a never-ending process that can help your business website to stand out from competition.

Each year, quite a few state-of-the-art techniques and strategies are being introduced that you can follow to reach your SEO goals and staying updated is mandatory. Let's uncover a few more SEO tips and tricks that you may adopt to help your business website boost its ranking on SERPs.

Website Speed

In order to achieve faster loading times for your business website, you can optimize and compress the images that you use. You can also discard any unnecessary HTTP requests or scripts.

Supervise Your Website's Performance

You can consider using an SEO analytics platform in order to keep track of your current performance. Google Analytics is a free all-encompassing SEO analytics platform which includes features that can help you understand where your traffic derives from, the amount of organic and paid traffic your business website receives and which of your web pages are the most trending.

Guide Users Skillfully

Keep your SEO goals in mind when you compose your content and don't forget to include call to actions, sales funnels, etc., that can help you to turn quality content into sales.

Internal Links Can Boost Usability

Use internal linking throughout your content - this will help your readers to click on other related content and stay engaged longer on your business website. By working this way, your previous content will be reused and strengthened with other new related articles and your readers can find other useful content to view.

Choose Your Words Wisely on Page Titles & Meta Descriptions

Your page titles and meta descriptions should allure users in SERPs. If you create appealing and intriguing page titles and meta descriptions, your CTR will probably skyrocket and your ranking will improve.

Automation of Social Media Posts

There are quite a few social media management platforms such as Hootsuite or Buffer that you can use to schedule your posts in advance and get real-time analytics to improve your social media presence. These tools can save you a considerable amount of time to schedule each post manually on each platform and additional costs as there are free plans to get started.

HTTPS Prevails

There is no doubt that HTTPS wins over HTTP. An SSL certificate lets your visitors know that there is an added level of security on your business website meaning that transactions and communications between your visitors and the server are encrypted.

Besides the fact that Google Chrome is now warning users when a website does not have an SSL certificate, having one can give your business website a small boost in rankings and help your brand to build trust with your customers.

Google My Business

This is a free and accessible tool for businesses as well as organizations to manage their online presence across Google. You can help your customers to locate you on Google Maps and inform them about your business, your hours of operation, your street address, your business website and about your products or services by verifying and editing your business information. You can also analyze data such as how many searchers called your business directly from the phone number displayed on local SERPs and Google Maps.

Create a Custom 404 Page

A 404 page is what users see when they try to enter a web page on your business website that does not exist. It might be a broken link, a web page that has been removed, or they have just mistyped a URL. Servers usually return a standard 404 page, but it is in most cases unappealing and without branding.

You can create a custom 404 page with your branding and provide helpful information and guidance to visitors that did not reach the web page they expected. You can include information about your brand, your most popular articles and internal links to web pages that they might find appealing and encourage them to explore more web pages on your business website. Ensure that your server returns a 404 HTTP status code when a missing web page is requested and try to hide this page from search results.

Keep Your SEO Plan Up-to-the-Minute

Keep in mind that there will always be further developments on how users search and how algorithms of search engines work; thus it is fundamental to keep track of the latest search engines' news that comes to light. Monitor your SEO performance and pay special attention to your visitors - invaluable content and powerful user experience should be your top priorities.

Additional SEO Resources & Tools

SEO Starter Guide by Google
https://support.google.com/webmasters/answer/7451184

Moz Beginner's Guide to SEO
https://moz.com/beginners-guide-to-seo

Advice, Research, How To, and Insights by The Moz Blog
https://moz.com/blog

Resources for content strategy and marketing, SEO, SEM, PPC, social media etc.
https://www.semrush.com/blog/

PageRank by Wikipedia
https://en.wikipedia.org/wiki/PageRank

Google Webmaster Tools (Search Console)
https://www.google.com/webmasters/tools/home?hl=en

Bing Webmaster Tools
http://www.bing.com/toolbox/webmaster

Google Analytics
https://www.google.com/analytics/

Google Trends
https://trends.google.com/trends/

PageSpeed Insights
https://developers.google.com/speed/pagespeed/insights/

Adwords Keyword Planner
https://adwords.google.com/intl/en/home/tools/keyword-planner/

Moz Keyword Explorer
https://moz.com/explorer

Keyword research and analysis tool by KWFinder
https://kwfinder.com/

FREE alternative to Google AdWords Keyword Planner for SEO & PPC keyword research
https://keywordtool.io/

Competitor Research Tools & SEO Backlink Checker by Ahrefs
https://ahrefs.com/

Search Engine Journal
https://www.searchenginejournal.com/

Search Engine Land
https://searchengineland.com/

A blog about analytics, marketing and testing
https://blog.kissmetrics.com/

Google My Business
https://www.google.com/business/

Facebook Business
https://www.facebook.com/business

Facebook Blueprint: Free Online Training for Advertising on Facebook
https://www.facebook.com/blueprint

Bing Places
https://www.bingplaces.com/

Yahoo Small Business
https://smallbusiness.yahoo.com/local

Yelp Listings
https://www.yelp.com/

SEO and search analytics software by SEMrush
https://www.semrush.com

Marketing Automation for E-Commerce Businesses by MailChimp
https://mailchimp.com/

Small SEO Tools
http://smallseotools.com/plagiarism-checker

Social Media Management by Buffer
https://buffer.com/

Social Media Management by Hootsuite
https://hootsuite.com/

Grow your audience and build a brand by Crowdfire
https://www.crowdfireapp.com/

Website Speed and Performance Optimization by GTmetrix
https://gtmetrix.com/

Plagiarism Checker by Copyscape
https://www.copyscape.com/

Free Writing Assistant by Grammarly
https://www.grammarly.com/

Check your Grammar and Proofread Online by Slick Write
https://www.slickwrite.com/

Create an XML Sitemap
https://www.xml-sitemaps.com/

Glossary of SEO Terms

1 – 100 | A | B | C | D | E | F | G | H | I | J | K | L | M | N | O | P | Q | R | S | T | U | V | W | X | Y | Z

301 Redirect: The HTTP response status code 301 is used for permanent URL redirection.

302 Redirect: The HTTP response status code 302 is used for temporary URL redirection. This redirect doesn't bear or give the link value to the new URL.

404 Page: 404 Not Found. This response code is generated when users attempt to follow a broken or dead link.

AdWords: This is an online advertising service developed by Google.

Affiliate Marketing: It refers to an advertising agreement where a business pays commission to third party websites to generate traffic or leads based on its referrals.

Alt Tag: This is an alternative text to an image which helps search engines and visually impaired users understand its context and description.

Analytics: Tool for SEO optimization and marketing purposes that can help you measure and track website traffic and gain insights about your visitors.

Anchor Text: It is the clickable text in a hyperlink, usually in blue color.

Authority Website: This is an established and valuable source of information.

Backlink: It is a link from some other website or blog.

Bing: This is Microsoft's web search engine.

Black Hat: SEO techniques that do not follow search engines rules.

Blog: This is a discussion or informational website which includes information in a chronological manner.

Bounce Rate: The percentage of visitors who enter a website and then exit without viewing any other web pages.

Business Listings: Also known as business directories, they are websites that list businesses with industry-based categories.

CMS: Content Management Systems support the formulation and adjustment of digital content.

Content (Text Copy): It is the written material created by copywriters to persuade readers to join an email list or buy products or services.

Content Marketing: This is a method of marketing focused on generating, and distributing content for a targeted audience online.

Conversion Rate: The percentage of website visitors that convert into customers.

CPC: Also known as Cost Per Click, it is a metric that helps advertisers to determine the cost of each click they pay when their ad is clicked.

CPM: It refers to the cost of traditional advertising or online marketing where advertisers pay every time an advertisement gets one thousand impressions.

CTR: Click Through Rate is the percentage of users who click on a specific link to the number of total users who view a web page, an email, or an advertisement.

Cloaking: This is an SEO method in which the content displayed to the search engine crawler is different from that displayed in the user's browser.

Crawlers: Also known as spiders, these are bots that methodically browse the internet to index websites in order to assist users to search more efficiently on search engines.

CSS: Cascading Style Sheets describes how HTML elements are to be presented on screen, paper, or in other media.

Deep Links: This is a hypertext link to a web page on a website other than its homepage.

Directory Submissions: It is the process of submitting a website on numerous business directories or online directories to generate backlinks.

Domain Age: It suggests the period of time that a website has been registered and operating.

DoFollow: Links that are followed by search engines spiders.

Duplicate Content: It describes content that shows up on more than one web page.

Dynamic URL: The returned URL of a database-driven website that executes a processing script while searching.

E-Commerce: It is the act of buying or selling of products or services online.

Flash: It is a multimedia software platform owned by Adobe Systems that is used to produce animation, advertisements, and miscellaneous web page elements.

Frames: These are independent parts of a web page which can load content separately.

Geotargeting: Process of identifying the geolocation of a website visitor and delivering distinct content to that visitor based on their location.

Googlebot: It is Google's crawling bot algorithm used to index and scan websites over the internet.

Heading Tag: Describes and inform search engines what a web page is about.

HTML: Hyper Text Markup Language is the leading markup language used to display web pages on the internet.

HTTP: HyperText Transfer Protocol is the fundamental protocol used by the World Wide Web to specify how information is formatted and transferred.

HTTPS: This is an extension of the HTTP for protected and encrypted communication between users and a website.

Hyperlink: A link that points to a complete document or to a specific section within a document.

Inbound Link: Hyperlink from a web page outside of your website that points to a web page on your website.

Index: A database that incorporates the information of all the websites that search engines were able to detect.

Internal Link: This is a hyperlink that points to another web page of the same website or domain.

JavaScript: It is a programming language regularly used in web development to generate interactive effects within web browsers.

Keywords: These are ideas and subjects that characterize what your content is about.

Keyword Density: The percentage of times a keyword or set of keywords appear on a web page in comparison to the total number of words on that web page.

Keyword Stuffing: It refers to the process of filling a web page with keywords in an attempt to manipulate a website's ranking in search engine results pages.

Landing Page: This is a single web page designed and written for a specific business goal.

Link Building: Technique which aims to increase the amount and quality of inbound links to a particular webpage in order to advance its rankings on search engines.

Link Exchange: Exchanging backlinks with other websites for link building purposes.

Link Farm: A website or an association of unrelated websites that hyperlink to every other for the purpose of increasing the number of incoming links with unquestionable negative effects for SEO and possible penalties from search engines.

Link Spam: A scheme of spamming to increase the number of outbound links made to a website for the purpose of promotion.

Local Search: Searching for websites that are relevant to a given location.

Meta Description: It is an HTML attribute that summarizes briefly a given web page.

Meta Keywords: These are embodied in the HTML code of a web page and indicate what the topic of a given web page is about.

Meta Tags: They integrate metadata about the HTML document such as keywords, page descriptions, date of last modification and other metadata.

Metrics: They help you to analyze the performance and success of your SEO strategy and include information about your organic traffic, bounce rate, conversion rate, keyword ranking, CTR, indexed pages, etc.

Navigation: It embodies all important elements about a website and helps visitors to browse other web pages and content within a website.

NoFollow: Links that are not followed by search engines spiders.

Organic Search: Traffic from search engine results pages that is generated naturally and not shaped by paid campaigns or online promotions.

Outbound Link: Hyperlink from a web page inside your website that points to a web page outside of your website.

Page Rank: This is Google's search algorithm that ranks websites in search engine results pages with a numeric value between 0 and 10.

Page Speed: It is the loading speed of a website.

Page Title: The primary text that describes a web page.

Paid Links: A paid followed backlink that points back to a website.

PPC: Also known as Cost Per Click, it is an online advertising model in which advertisers pay when their advertisement is clicked.

Proximity (Keywords): It refers to the distance between the search term and the title of a website. Imagine website A with title "Create resume for free online", website B with title "Create resume using our free online platform" and the search term "resume online". Distance between words "resume" and "online" on website A is 2, whereas on website B is 3. Proximity is greater on website A.

Reciprocal Links: These are backlinks between two niche-related websites who encompass complementary topics, products or services.

Robots.txt: A file that consists of one or more rules which is used by crawlers to index web content.

RSS Feed: Rich Site Summary Feed incorporates headlines, updates and notifications about web content delivered directly to subscribers.

Sandbox: It is a testing environment that limits system deficiency or unverified third party software vulnerabilities from spreading.

Search Engine: A complex algorithm that looks for and identifies pieces of information in a database that match terms specified by a searcher.

<u>SEO</u>: Search Engine Optimization is the technique of increasing the online discoverability, quantity and quality of organic traffic and ranking on search engine results pages to a website.

<u>SERP</u>: Abbreviation for Search Engine Results Page. It is the page presented by a search engine in response to a search input by a searcher.

<u>Sitemap</u>: The list of web pages of a website.

<u>SLD</u>: Second Level Domain is the domain name that we usually purchase at domain name registrars and web hosting companies.

<u>Social Media</u>: Websites and platforms where you can create and share thoughts, images or videos or engage in virtual communities and networks.

<u>SMM</u>: Social Media Marketing involves both organic and paid marketing strategies on social media platforms to drive quality traffic to a website and increase sales.

<u>Spiders</u>: Also known as crawlers, they are software programs that are used systematically by search engines to scan and index web content.

<u>Splash Page</u>: This is the first page of a website that visitors view before proceeding to the main website and it is essentially used to advertise a business, a distinguishing product or service or provides worthwhile information to visitors.

SSL: Secure Sockets Layer is the definitive technology to maintain an internet connection safe and to shield any sensitive data such as credit card transactions, data transmissions and logins secure.

Static URL: A URL that is changeless, understandable and does not alter depending on data from a database or server.

Title Tag: This is an HTML attribute that describes the title of a web page.

TLD: A Top Level Domain describes the broadest part of a domain name and it is the extension that appears at the end of an internet address.

URL Rewrite: It is the procedure of modifying the parameters in a Uniform Resource Locator (URL) to enchase the usability and discoverability of your website.

White Hat: Search engine optimization strategies and techniques that target on a human audience rather than search engines and comply with search engine's rules and policies.

WWW: Abbreviation for World Wide Web